Don DeLillo's
White Noise

CONTINUUM CONTEMPORARIES

Also available in this series

Forthcoming in this series

· DON DELILLO'S

White
Noise

A READER'S GUIDE

LEONARD ORR

CONTINUUM | NEW YORK | LONDON

2003

The Continuum International Publishing Group Inc
370 Lexington Avenue, New York, NY 10017

The Continuum International Publishing Group Ltd
The Tower Building, 11 York Road, London SE1 7NX

www.continuumbooks.com

Printed in the United States of America

Library of Congress Cataloging-in-Publication Data

Orr, Leonard, 1953–
    Don Delillo's White noise : a reader's guide / Leonard Orr.
       p.   cm.—(Continuum contemporaries)
    Includes bibliographical references (p.   ).
    ISBN 0-8264-1474-5 (pbk. : alk. paper)
    1. Delillo, Don. White noise.   I. Title: White noise.   II. Title.   III.
Series.
PS3554.E4425W4837   2003
813'.54—dc21   2003003731

Contents

The Novelist

Although Don DeLillo began publishing fiction in the 1960s, and his first novel appeared in 1971, he was not on the lists of major contemporary American authors until *White Noise* appeared in 1985. He had achieved a number of enthusiastic critical notices, and some harsh attacks, for his novels of the seventies, but he had small sales and little public attention. It must be said, he did not court the public or the press. He did not grant interviews (in an often-told anecdote, potential interviewers who approached DeLillo were handed a printed card that said "I do not want to talk about it"). He did not go on any publicity tour until the publication of *Libra* (1988), he did not appear on television talk shows, he didn't teach creative writing at a university. But *White Noise*, DeLillo's eighth novel, was an unexpected commercial success, selling 300,000 copies. While his other novels were satires (sometimes structured under the guise of some other popular genre such as the spy novel or a sports novel), *White Noise* was his most accessible book, less complexly structured, more traditional and realistic in its portrayal of American life than his other works, and his funniest book. Dealing with many different issues from technology to ecological disaster, satirizing institutions from the modish university to the contemporary family (with multiple marriages and divorces and fractional siblings and parents), *White Noise* immediately became a popular text for university literature courses.

Now there is no doubt about DeLillo's lasting significance as a writer. In the second half of his writing career, DeLillo's work has received substantial critical recognition and he has been given many honors and awards. He was made a member of the American Academy of Arts and Letters which gave him their Award in Literature in 1984, he won the National Book Award for *White Noise* (1985), the Aer Lingus/*Irish Times* International Fiction Prize for *Libra* (1989), the PEN/Faulkner Award for *Mao II* (1991), and the Lila Wallace-*Reader's Digest* Award (1995). The publication of *Underworld* in particular has placed him in a position where critics have spoken of DeLillo as a contender for the Nobel Prize. *Underworld* received the Jerusalem Prize (1999) (for a "writer whose work expresses the theme of the freedom of the individual in society"), the Riccardo Bacchelli International Award (2000), and the American Academy of Arts and Letters William Dean Howells Medal (2000; this prize is awarded every five years for the "most distinguished work of American fiction published during the previous five years").

DeLillo, born November 20, 1936, grew up in an Italian-American neighborhood of the Bronx where he enjoyed Catholicism because of its theatrical, aesthetic aspects, and because it dealt with "big" issues and questions. Although this background rarely surfaces in the novels, glimpses can be seen in DeLillo's short stories published in the 1960s, especially "The River Jordan," "Take the 'A' Train," and "Spaghetti and Meatballs," and does not return to the Italian-American neighborhood in his fiction until some sections of *Underworld*.

His father immigrated from Italy in 1916, at the age of nine, and DeLillo has said little about him except that he worked for Metropolitan Life Insurance in a large office with hundreds of identical desks as some sort of auditor. He claims to have gotten little out his formal education, claiming to have slept through Cardinal Hayes High School and then Fordham University ("I didn't study much of anything. I majored in something called 'communication arts'"). He has said in a number of interviews that the street games were more influential for him than any literature he encountered. Most recently, in a 2002 interview for the collection *Books that Changed My Life*, he said that when he was young he did not read at all but spent his time playing "street games, card games, alley games, rooftop games, fire escape games, punchball, stickball, handball, stoop ball." But he mentions reading on his own, as a teenager, Walt Whitman, James T. Farrell's Studs Lonigan trilogy, and fiction by William Faulkner, Ernest Hemingway, James Joyce, and Herman Melville. Joyce is probably the name he has mentioned most often in reference to his early reading, and he has used Stephen Dedalus's words from *A Portrait of the Artist as a Young Man* ("silence, exile, and cunning") on more than a few occasions in response to questions about his reclusive habits. Thomas Pynchon is the contemporary novelist for whom he has shown the greatest respect, using Pynchon's *Gravity's Rainbow* as a benchmark for measuring what the novel can achieve. But more than literary influence, DeLillo has spoken about the impact of the other arts, especially the jazz of Charles Mingus and Miles Davis, abstract expressionist painting, and foreign films from directors such as Federico Fellini and the French *nouvelle vague* cinema of the 1960s, in particular the films of Jean-Luc Godard.

After graduating from Fordham, DeLillo worked as an advertising copywriter for Ogilvy and Mather (a career he has described as short and uninteresting) while beginning to develop his stories and his first novel. In 1964 he decided to devote himself completely to writing, and he left his advertising work after about five years (yet De-

Lillo claims, "I quit my job just to quit. I didn't quit my job to write fiction. I just didn't want to work anymore"). He worked on his first novel, *Americana* (1971), with frequent interruptions to write free-lance non-fiction. Ascetic and serious, in these first years of his writing career DeLillo lived in a tiny apartment with a refrigerator in the bathroom and no stove. He has said in interviews that he first began to feel that he was a writer only when he was working on the second half of *Americana*. In his 1993 *Paris Review* interview with Adam Begley, DeLillo explained the sort of interior change he underwent in becoming a novelist:

Even when I was well into my first novel I didn't have a system for working, a dependable routine. I worked haphazardly, sometimes late at night, some-times in the afternoon. I spent too much time doing other things or nothing at all. On humid summer nights I tracked horseflies through the apartment and killed them—not for the meat but because they were driving me crazy with their buzzing. I hadn't developed a sense of the level of dedication that's necessary to do this kind of work.

DeLillo's Novels before White Noise

Although DeLillo's novels are always violating formal and generic expectations, they return repeatedly to a group of themes, patterns, and images. DeLillo's readers find a small thematic vocabulary turning on (1) the media (television, film, and advertising), resonant with DeLillo's major in "communication arts" and his unhappy career in advertising copywriting; (2) major events such as the assassination of John F. Kennedy, the Cold War, and the race to accumulate stockpiles of nuclear weapons; (3) terrorism, spying, violence, and governmental control and excesses; (4) waste, pollution, toxic substances, and the relationship of science, power, authority, and discourse; and (5) the heteroglossia of different languages, jargons, clichés, social and cultural registers of speech, and all of the signifying systems of culture observed and described minutely, employing all of the ranges of styles that are appropriate to the diversity of the subject matter. Thirty-two years after DeLillo's first novel was published, we can see that what reviewers attacked him for doing in that book and those following (i.e., that the novels lack form, a clear, recognizable plot and closure, that there are no three-dimensional characters, that the prose is sloppy) may be seen now as deliberate, precise, the result of great effort by someone deeply engaged in contemporary issues.

David Bell, the main character of *Americana* (1971), DeLillo's first novel, is a television network executive who dreams of making a film modeled on the work of experimental French directors such as Jean-Luc Godard and François Truffaut. The son of a television advertising pioneer, Clinton Bell, who obsessively watched and analyzed commercials with his son, David Bell has difficulty now seeing outside the movie theater and the television. Having spent the first twenty-eight years of his life "in the movies," he regards being filmed and viewed as essential to giving meaning to life, or even as a means of knowing that a life existed. The representation has greater reality than what is represented, a topic echoed in *White Noise*, *Libra*, and *Underworld*. He sees that his parents, in particular his father who could not accept anything that did not match permanently the perfect filmed image (such as David's mother), are his main subject matter, and he proceeds from an image of an older woman trimming a hedge, recognizing his attraction to older women as an oedipal plot. David makes his film with a handheld camera, like Godard, with actors playing his parents and David acting as a director who also acts within his film in order not to make a commercial film, but to understand his own psychodrama. He ends in isolation on an island, viewing his film repeatedly, unable to stop.

End Zone (1972) might seem to be about college football, but it is actually about language, power, violence, the Cold War, and nuclear weapons. Focused on the football team of Coach Emmett Creed, whose sole purpose is winning no matter through what means or how self-destructive, the story is located in the West Texas campus of Logos College. (*Logos* itself is a charged term for language, reason, and spirit, with Christian theological meaning, and is an important term in Martin Heidegger's existential philosophy, and that connection adds further complication because of Heidegger's support of Nazism in the 1930s). The novel foregrounds the language of aggression, anti-Semitism, racism, sexism, war, destruction, the military, and the atomic bomb. Similarly, DeLillo's third novel, *Great Jones Street* (1973), seems to be about famous political rock star Bucky Wunderlick and his sudden withdrawal from the spotlight because he realizes that his protest songs have unintentionally been the source of violence, but it's actually more about language, the ubiquity and saturation of society by the media, and the commodification of the celebrity.

Ratner's Star (1976) is a sharp departure in style and genre from DeLillo's earlier works. Centered on fourteen-year-old math genius Billy Twillig, *Ratner's Star* has been called everything from a science fiction novel to a Menippean satire; from a mathematical allegory to, simply, an "experimental novel." Harshly attacked by many reviewers because of its complexity and lack of traditional realism, DeLillo said in an interview that "The structure of the book *is* the book. The characters are intentionally flattened and cartoonlike. I was trying to build a novel which was not only about mathematics to some extent but which itself would become a piece of mathematics. . . . The people had to play a role subservient to pattern, form, and so on. This is difficult, of course, for all concerned, but I believed I was doing something new and was willing to take the risk" (DeCurtis 1991: 59). Working in a think tank called Field Experiment Number

One, Billy Twillig is obsessively disturbed by waste, toxic materials, bodily functions and products. Billy and the scientists are also much filled with fear of death, the phobia that is so prominent in *White Noise*. Like *Great Jones Street*, *Ratner's Star* is also about multinational conglomerates and globalization; as in *White Noise*, there is a relationship between technology and fascism.

DeLillo's next three novels take on some aspects of the thriller or spy novel, while revealing a complex interplay between the media, marketing, terrorism, language, and power. Disaffected Wall Street broker Lyle Wynant in *Players* (1977), whose work and marriage are mechanical, constantly infused by television, becomes involved with a secret terrorist organization and then becomes a double-agent informing the FBI about the activities of the terrorists (even as he has affairs). Everything is marked by ambiguity, duplicity, and television imagery that he imitates, and he fantasizes about his multiple roles, finally unable to know what reality is. Unintentionally ironic, Lyle's wife Pammy works for the Grief Management Council located in the World Trade Center. In *Running Dog* (1978), Glen Selvy works as a spy for a private group called Radial Matrix that was apparently an offshoot of the CIA, while his overt job is as an assistant to Lloyd Percival, a US Senator who is a greedy collector of pornography, and that is a cover for his covert job for the senator, overseeing the pornography collection and working with dealers so that the senator can stay at a distance. Most of the novel deals with shady collectors, dealers, and underground groups trying to locate a film shot in Hitler's bunker in Berlin during the closing weeks of World War II that is said to be very erotic, involving possibly Hitler himself, that has recently surfaced. The combination of Nazism and the iconic figure of Hitler, secrecy, illicit sexuality, the desire to possess items for a collection, the monetary value of such a rarity, make this film the most coveted object. When the film is finally shown, it reveals Hitler in the bunker doing a comical imitation of Charlie Chaplin imitating Hitler in his 1940 film *The Great Dictator*. James Axton, in *The Names* (1982), travels to third-world countries gathering information for risk analyses so that his insurance company can insure American executives against assassination or guerilla attacks. But his company secretly is part of the CIA. *The Names* brilliantly unveils the rhetoric and means of imperialism and post-colonialism, and the interconnection of globalized, multi-national corporations; like Lyle Wynant in *Players*, James Axton unexpectedly becomes caught up in a murder cult that selects victims according to alphabetic coincidences whose story is told by James' son Tap.

White Noise *and After*

From 1979 through 1982, DeLillo, supported by a Guggenheim Fellowship, lived in Greece and traveled through Europe and the Middle East. This change in perspective, life in non-English-speaking cultures, and then a return to an America that seemed transformed in his absence, had a tremendous impact on DeLillo, and it altered the type of fiction that he wrote. "I lived abroad for three years, and when I came back to this country in 1982, I began to notice something on television which I hadn't noticed before. This was the daily toxic spill—there was the news, the weather, and the toxic spill. This was a phenomenon no one even mentioned. It was simply a television reality. It's only the people who were themselves involved who seemed to be affected by them. No one even talked about them. This was one of the motivating forces of *White Noise*" (DeLillo, interview with Rothstein, 1987). The 1980s saw one ecological and technological disaster after another: the meltdown at the Chernobyl nuclear power plant in 1986, the Exxon Valdez oil tanker spill off the coast of Alaska in 1989, and, just a few months before the publication of *White Noise*, the worst event in terms of human life: the December 1984 release of toxic gas from the Union Carbide Plant in Bhopal, India. The International Medical Commission on Bhopal estimated that there were 2000 casualties and 100,000 injuries; ten years after the accident, about 50,000 people remained fully or partially disabled as a result.

After *Running Dog* and *The Names*, *White Noise*, winner of the American Book Award, came as a surprise for readers and reviewers of DeLillo's work. Though filled with humor and working with many of the same themes and issues as his earlier works (television and the blurring distinctions between reality and the filmed reproduction, advertising, consumerism, waste and pollution, globalization, violence, and fear of death), *White Noise* has an appealing, straightforward surface. It seems like a more traditional novel, though we will see in Chapter 2 that it is more complicated than that. It is a family novel, even if that family is dispersed and the result of multiple marriages and divorces, with ex-spouses and children around the world, with half-siblings and step-children and step-parents in the household. It seems like a campus novel, with its conventions of genial satire of academic fads and eccentric professors, even though it has violent scenes graphically described, toxic gas that plants death in the protagonist, and overwhelming fears of dying. The structure is simple: a first section called "Waves and Radiation" that reveals, with brilliant mimicry, the interactions of the family members, the hilarious on-campus workings of the Jack Gladney (who seems to have no colleagues in Hitler Studies) and the American Environments faculty. The central section is euphemistically titled "The Airborne Toxic Event" with Jack's exposure to the perhaps-deadly plume. The third section, "Dylarama," a name that combines the high-tech, unapproved drug that can remove the fear of death with a marketer's or huckster's suffix. But the generic and plot expectations are continually undone throughout the novel, and the ending perhaps leaves everything in complete disorder and confusion, like the impact of the rearranged goods in the supermarket.

DeLillo followed this critical and best-selling success with the much more bristly *Libra* (1988). The novel is about Lee Harvey Oswald and an investigation into his life and the assassination of John F. Kennedy by a retired CIA analyst, Nicholas Branch, first seen in his fifteenth year of work on the project, a room filled with books and documents, "the room of theories and dreams." Here we have all the conspiracy theories, especially one leading back to Win Everett, also a former CIA employee, an agent involved in training Cuban exiles for the 1961 Bay of Pigs disaster. Everett came up with the scheme of making an attempt on President Kennedy's life and letting the evidence lead to Cuban dictator Fidel Castro in the hopes of prompting an invasion of the island. There is great attention to detail, both biographical fragments showing Oswald and his Russian-born wife, and historical. But this *Libra* is not a satirical excursion along the lines of Robert Coover's *The Public Burning*, which used Richard Nixon as a narrator, nor is it an attempt to recreate events exactly based on exhaustive research. DeLillo commented that he didn't read more than a quarter of the twenty-six-volume Warren Commission Report on the assassination. Like the acclaimed and disturbing British novelist J. G. Ballard, DeLillo has said several times that the Warren Commission Report had a certain fascination, and was in fact a sort of postmodern novel. DeLillo was shrilly and famously attacked by George Will who felt that he was glorifying Oswald. DeLillo is sharply focused on the media, especially news film and television, but also in the way Oswald imitated, and was aware of, photographs and films of his heroes, such as Lenin, and emulated them, and the impossibility of Branch's attempts to piece everything together using such piles of documentation.

Mao II (1991) is another novel about celebrity and commodification, about the intrusive nature of the media, about the role of the author in contemporary American society. Bill Gray is a much celebrated novelist who has been attempting to escape his position as a cultural hero, becoming a recluse in the manner of J. D. Salinger or Thomas Pynchon. As with those figures, becoming reclusive just increases the desire of people to see him, find information about him, and his books with his name stand for him (Pynchon provided a praise-filled blurb for the book). Bill Gray has only written two short books, and many details about his writing habits and statements about writing coincide with DeLillo's own views. The other aspect of *Mao II* that is especially linked with *White Noise* is the depiction of crowds and the attempt to conform, to share the same perceptions and views as a mass of people (*Mao II* begins with thousands of brides and grooms in a stadium joining in a mass marriage ceremony conducted by Reverend Sun-yung Moon of the Unification Church through satellite and a large-screen television). One has to recall Jack Gladney's course in Advanced Nazism that focused on Hitler's massive rallies and filmed scenes of crowds, the manipulation of symbols, uniforms, spectacles, and the forms of mass submission.

DeLillo's most acclaimed novel to date is *Underworld* (1997); at 827 pages, it is his longest and most complex work (subject of an excellent study in this series by John Duvall). Like *White Noise*, it carries the themes of waste and recycling not only through Nick Shay who owns an enormous waste-recycling business, but through the artist who is making artworks in the Tucson desert out of the long-retired airplanes that have been left there, and through the collectors of baseball memorabilia. *Underworld* is about celebrity, history, and media with scenes depicting Frank Sinatra and Jackie Gleason in 1951, with J. Edgar Hoover, director of the FBI, manipulating the way reporters and cameras would show him and the Bureau. It is about the Cold War, technology, and crowds (especially the crowd at a baseball game in 1951, or the audiences of television). The work moves about in time from the fifties to the nineties, and allows DeLillo full scope to show his range of styles and precise accumulation of detail.

More recently, DeLillo published a completely different sort of work, not much longer than a novella, *The Body Artist* (2001), a minimalist work with just a handful of characters. We see a woman, Lauren, who is a performance artist, a modern expressive dancer, and her older husband Rey as they have breakfast and talk, but not connecting very much in their dialogue, then learn from a newspaper article that Rey was Spanish, a film director, and he has committed suicide in the apartment of his first wife; Lauren is his third wife. Then we have the widowed dancer's memories and observations of daily life. With such an inventive and prolific author as DeLillo, one hopes for many more novels; the latest work announced at the time of this writing is *Cosmopolis* (to appear in April, 2003).

Other writing

DeLillo has often examined urgent public issues in his non-fiction, and these matters are developed in his fiction. His "American Blood: A Journey Through the Labyrinth of Dallas and JFK," appeared in *Rolling Stone* in 1983, and this is explored in the novel *Libra*. Although he is often described as reclusive, he participated in group letters in defense of Salman Rushdie in 1989 and 1994 after the Iranian revolutionary leader Ayatollah Kohmeini issued a *fatwa* or religious death sentence against Rushdie because of the novel *Satanic Verses*. In 1989 DeLillo wrote a fairly scholarly piece on Nazism and millenarianism, taking up issues from *Running Dog* and *White Noise*, in the magazine of B'nai Brith. He also delivered a speech,

"The Artist Naked in Cage," for the Chinese writer Wei Jingsheng, at the New York Public Library's event for Human Rights in China. More recently, after the September 11, 2001 terrorist attacks on the World Trade Center and Pentagon, DeLillo published an essay called "In the Ruins of the Future," in *Harper's* on terrorist events, terrorism, technology, and the impact on America. He has also published a number of short stories (not yet collected), and has written a few plays, some of them very short, and at least two of these have been performed.

2

The Novel

Family

More so than any of his novels before or since, *White Noise* is a traditional, realistic, domestic novel, focused on a single, middle-class family, a typical American town. It is not only the setting for many contemporary American novels, but it is in the nineteenth-century tradition of Jane Austen and George Eliot. As Tom LeClair noted, "While writing *White Noise*, DeLillo mocked what he called the 'around-the-house-and-in-the-yard' school of American fiction, a realism about 'marriages and separations and trips to Tanglewood' that gives its readers' reflected lives 'a certain luster, a certain significance'" (LeClair, 1987: p. 208). Though the "Airborne Toxic Event" is the central section of the book's tripartite structure, this event is framed by the Gladney family and their responses to each other and to the impact of the "events" of the world entering their lives through all different medium.

But DeLillo's American family of the 1980s is far removed either from the Victorian tradition or, what might come more immediately to mind, the television sit-com family of the 1960s and 70s. The Gladneys straddle the traditional and the contemporary family situation in complex ways. In this household there are two adults and four children, middle-class and comfortable residents of a small, university town. The father is the "breadwinner," with a respectable position as a tenured professor and with some international academic fame as the founder of Hitler Studies. The mother does volunteer work, food shopping, and she exercises to lose weight. On the other hand, Jack and Babette have each been married four times, their children all have different parents, and some of the children live with former spouses of Jack or Babette in foreign countries (see Thomas Ferraro on all of the complexities of family relationships in the Gladney household, and how that information is conveyed: Ferraro, 1991: pp. 16–17).

The information about the dispersed Gladney family, including the former spouses and non-resident children, is not given in one long passage of exposition, but is spread through the novel, so the first appearance makes the family seem more solid and home-centered than it is. Before Babette, Jack's marriages were all to women in the "intelligence community" (Dana Breedlove, Janet Savory, Tweedy Browner, and Dana Breedlove again), all high-strung, nervous women who received mysterious phone calls and spoke in foreign languages and took sudden trips they didn't discuss. Jack speculates, "Some of my adoration of Babette must have been sheer relief" (WN, pp. 203–4). One of Jack's former wives, Heinrich's mother, has become Mother Devi and lives in the ashram of Dharamsalapur, once merely Tubb, Montana, where she takes care of the financial side of her swami's empire. One of Babette's sons lives with his father in the Australian outback, a place so remote he has never watched television (on the family see LeClair 1987: 208–9, 216–17). We learn small pieces of information about these far-flung relations when one of the former spouses visits the Gladneys, when Babette's ex-husband Bob Pardee, who raises money for a legal defense fund for the nuclear industry, suddenly appears at the house, or when there is a phone call from thousands of miles away and Jack imagines the voice of his wife translated into a digital signal and bounced from ground station to satellite and back to earth (see Peyser on the way *WN* is on the one hand the most domestic and most focused on family of any of DeLillo's novels, and on the other hand, thoroughly involved in globalization, even within the extended Gladney family [Peyser, 1996: pp. 267–68]).

Perhaps because of this decentering, Jack and Babette offer little direction in the family. As Mark Conroy has noted, "One suspects its family tree would have many branches but no trunk. The parent figures ('parents' seems not to indicate the role properly) are Jack and his wife Babette; but they do none of the passing on of wisdom that is supposed to be older generation's portion. Instead, the television seems to be the chief source of information and even guidance . . ." (Conroy, 1994: p. 98; see also Ferraro, 1991: pp. 24–29). The repeated family scene in *WN* is one of confusion, misinformation, uncertainty, and irony.

The introductory gathering of the family captures this, as everyone is milling about in the kitchen separately yet simultaneously looking for something to eat, pulling out all different foods and leaving the counters and table covered with shredded packaging and the inedible remains of food. The children make fun of Babette's strategy of buying healthy foods such as yogurt that she never eats because it makes her feel healthier just putting it in her cart, while Jack thinks he prefers Babette's bulkiness, that it is part of the definition of "Babette." This is what passes for the family meal (*WN*, p. 7). Jack wanders the house taking pleasure in his sleeping children and is confused by what they say and do when they are awake, always wondering whether he should say anything that might influence a decision when the children are not fully his. He then dresses in his costume as J. A. K. Gladney, professor of Hitler Studies, hidden inside his academic regalia, dark glasses, and his own bulkiness and heads to campus ("I am the false character that follows the name around" [WN, pp. 16–17]). Babette is similarly confused in conversation with her children, but spends her spare time teaching community courses in topics like walking, standing, and eating, or else reading the tabloid newspapers to blind Mr. Treadwell. Babette attempts to establish a family tradition of having a family meal once a week with the enticements of eating Chinese takeout food and watching television; she has the reasonable belief that having the children watch television with their parents will de-glamorize television. But she cannot keep them to watching the rare "wholesome" shows; as soon as someone learns that "disaster footage" is on, it causes everyone to rush out to watch on another television.

Listening to the Gladneys trading inaccurate guesses about the meaning of Dylar, the experimental drug that removes the fear of death, is emblematic of the way the family discusses all matters. Jack thinks, "The family is the cradle of the world's misinformation. There must be something in family life that generates factual error."

"What do you know about Dylar?"

"Is that the black girl who's staying with the Stovers?"

"That's Dakar," Steffie said.

"Dakar isn't her name, it's where she's from," Denise said. It's a country on the ivory coast of Africa."

"The capital is Lagos," Babette said. "I know that because of a surfer movie I saw once where they travel all over the world." [. . . .]

"They go to Hawaii," Denise told Steffie, "and wait for these tidal waves to come from Japan. They're called origamis."

"And the movie was called *The Long Hot Summer*," her mother said.

"*The Long Hot Summer*," Heinrich said, "happens to be a play by Tennessee Ernie Williams." (WN, pp. 80–81).

There are similar conversations about whether a rat is a vermin, a rodent, or a mammal, wondering whether astronauts can float because they are lighter than air, and the conversation that begins with government psychics, UFOs, and why mountains are always upstate, or the argument about the skin damage caused by the rays of the sun and whether runners are less likely to be hit by the rays than walkers or people standing still (WN, pp. 121, 220–25, 252). But Jack and Babette engage in these conversations as equals or even backward learners compared with their children, and Jack, the professor, is often persuaded by the argument, or at least is too confused to speak authoritatively on any subject. Mark Conroy has observed that Heinrich, not Jack, "is the closest thing the family has to a repository of learning, because he is 'plugged in' to things scientific" (Conroy, 1994: p. 98). When Heinrich describes all of the elements of the environment to be fearful about, all types of radiation, electric and magnetic fields, Babette and Jack respond to this by trying, pathetically, to remember the factoids given to them in their student days: "The square of the hypotenuse is equal to the sum of the squares of the two sides. The battle of Bunker Hill was really fought on Breed's Hill. Here's one. Latvia, Estonia and Lithuania." " 'Was it the *Monitor* or the *Merrimac* that got sunk?' I said. 'I don't know but it was Tippecanoe and Tyler too.' " (WN, p. 168).

Heinrich, a fourteen-year-old, serves as both the scientific authority who has stored up information on matters ranging from dangers of electromagnetic transmissions to animal sexual behavior to the particular qualities of the gas that forms the toxic cloud in the central section of the novel, Nyodene Derivative. He seems to be balding, and he is usually removed from the family conversations except to provide alternative misinformation that the rest of the family finds persuasive. He is constantly listening to the radio, watching television, alert to disaster footage, and he plays chess by mail with an imprisoned mass murderer. At the start of the Airborne Toxic Event, he is up on the roof, dressed in camouflage and carrying binoculars, and his strongest fifteen minutes in the book takes place when he gives an impromptu lecture on Nyodene D. for the terrified and baffled evacuees craving information. Jack admires the transformation of Heinrich from a quiet and reclusive teenager into a relaxed and professional-sounding authority and he doesn't stand where Heinrich can see him to avoid interfering with this brief period of triumph.

At the same time that Heinrich places faith in scientific knowledge and discourse, he is skeptical about information, the media, and the senses. In the car with Jack on a rainy day, he will not acknowledge that it is raining because the radio said it would be raining that evening (WN, pp. 23–24). Jack points out the rain hitting the windshield and says, "Just because it's on the radio doesn't mean we have to suspend belief in the evidence of our senses," to which Heinrich responds, "Our senses? Our senses are wrong a lot more often than they're right. This has been proved in the laboratory." Jack continues trying to get Heinrich to admit that it is raining, only to have Heinrich question the existence of absolute truth, the meaning of "now," "here," and "rain."

Occasionally, Jack and Heinrich do share a perspective or interest and it leads to a sudden moment of father-son bonding, as when they discuss Heinrich's acquaintance, Orestes Mercator, whose obsessive goal is to stay in a cage filled with venomous snakes in order to make it into the *Guinness Book of World Records.* "'Every time I see newsfilm of someone in his fourth week of sitting in a cage full of snakes, I find myself wishing he'd get bitten.' 'So do I.' 'Why is that?' 'He's asking for it.' 'That's right. Most of us spend our lives avoiding danger. Who do these people think they are?' 'They ask for it. Let them get it.' I paused for a while, savoring the rare moment of agreement" (WN, p. 174). Another rare moment of camaraderie comes when Jack and Heinrich spend the night watching the insane asylum burn down and afterwards Jack fixes warm milk for them both (WN, pp. 228–29).

While children are not that common as characters in DeLillo's fiction, they seem invested with symbolic significance whenever they occur. DeLillo has said, in his interview with DeCurtis, "I think we feel, perhaps superstitiously, that children have a direct route to, have direct contact with the kind of natural truth that eludes us as adults. In *The Names* the father is transported by what he sees as a kind of deeper truth underlying the language his son uses in writing his stories. He sees misspellings and misused words as reflecting a kind of reality that he, as an adult, couldn't possibly grasp." David Cowart notes that in *Americana*, DeLillo's first novel, the child as a symbol of betrayed innocence becomes a repeated image in DeLillo's fiction, "an idea of the redemptive innocence that survives, a vestige of Eden, in children. The boy with the lantern, an almost inchoate symbol here, will turn up again as the linguistically atavistic Tap in *The Names* and as Wilder on his tricycle in *White Noise*" (Cowart, 2002: p. 143; see also p. 167). This attitude toward children, surprisingly Rousseauistic (the Romantic, Noble Savage, primitivist), is exemplified by the inarticulate, inexplicable, youngest Gladney. Appropriately named, Wilder brings comfort to the death-phobic parents, and is of anthropological interest to Murray Siskind. Wilder is free from fear because he has no foreknowledge of death, as shown through primitive responses to the supermarket and to Babette on television.

Despite their constant talk and their ongoing analysis of the events and the media, the Gladneys seem baffled by Wilder's silence. In contrast with his sometimes uncomprehending relationship with his older children, Jack feels comforted by Wilder, and seems to understand him. Jack says, "I liked being with Wilder. The world was a series of fleeting gratifications. He took what he could, then immediately forgot it in a rush of a subsequent pleasure. It was this forgetfulness I envied and admired" (*WN*, p. 162; see the analysis of Wilder, in contrast to the rest of the Gladney family, Cowart,

2002: pp. 81–82). Wilder wanders off unnoticed in the supermarket, or he is simply forgotten, and he mainly appears as a silent watcher. But he is the center of a few key episodes. One day, inexplicably, he cries for many hours and will not respond to his parents' attempts to calm and cheer him. They cannot find anything wrong with him, and they can't decide about bringing him to the doctor for something like crying. When Wilder abruptly stops crying, this is as confusing as the original cause (WN, pp. 75–79). When Babette appears on television, the other members of the family stare transfixed by Babette's transcendence while Wilder alone is calm. Everyone else in the family loses interest and leaves as the picture is lost while Wilder is left alone softly crying, grieving before the dark screen for the loss of his mother, while Murray Siskind takes notes (WN, pp. 102–4). But the moment with Wilder that has attracted the most critical attention is his miraculous escape from death when, near the end of the novel, he rides his plastic tricycle into the middle of traffic on the highway, and then he is rescued (WN, pp. 306–8).

How should we understand Wilder's tricycle ride? Ellen Pifer has a positive spin on this scene: it is about the community joining together to rescue the child in need of protection (Pifer, 2000: pp. 30–32). Tom LeClair sees the entire episode of the tricycle ride as a measurement of the changes that have taken place in Jack since his exposure to the Nyodene, his confrontation with death and his violent plot with his wife's sexual partner ("lover" seems not an accurate word for the Dylar and television-addled Willy Mink); the most notable sign of this change is Jack's failure to analyze the event (LeClair, 1987: p. 223). Mark Conroy thinks that Jack's inclusion of the episode in his story is a sign that he has interpreted the safe passage of Wilder and his miraculous return as a "good omen," showing that Jack "has indeed succumbed to superstition, as well as the final instance of that recurrent DeLillo chiasmus whereby adults look to their children for guidance" (Conroy, 1994: p. 110, n7). David

Cowart argues that the Wilder's tricycle ride and rescue from the expressway traffic, "ostensibly a picture of childhood insouciance in the face of death, is really the ironically negative index of just how far into the dread those fully initiated into *timor mortis*—Wilder's parents, for example—have strayed." For Cowart, it is one of a series of allegorical tableaux at the end of the novel: the sunsets after the Airborne Toxic Event, first modern and then postmodern, reminiscent of Oswald Spengler's metaphor of the decline of the west; the supermarket at the end no longer the place of fulfillment and excitement, but of baffled decline, confusion, and shoppers lining up at "terminals" on their way to "check out" (Cowart, 2000: pp. 81, 90).

Death and Fear

Death is everywhere in *White Noise*. One of DeLillo's working titles for the novel was *The American Book of the Dead*. Murray Siskind discusses the *Tibetan Book of the Dead*, and Jack's German tutor has been reading a German translation of the *Egyptian Book of the Dead*. The central event of the book is the Airborne Toxic Event, Heinrich's acquaintance Orestes Mercator wants to get into the *Guinness Book* by defying death through sitting in a glass cage filled with deadly snakes, and Heinrich plays chess with a convicted mass killer. Jack's academic specialty focuses on the major architect of genocide, while Murray Siskind and his colleagues in the American Environments program are obsessed with the nostalgia connected with the deaths of celebrities and the assassinations of politicians, and the representation of death in popular culture, such as Murray's course on car crashes in American film.

Death is part of the white noise that seeps in with the sounds from the nearby highway: "traffic washes past, a remote and steady murmur around our sleep, as of dead souls babbling at the edge of a dream" (WN, p. 4). Noises of activity and technology bring death to mind. Ironically, the only place of silence in the entire book, a place that draws Jack in baffled and meditative nostalgia, is the old burying ground. It is a place left out of modern culture, on the fringe of Blacksmith, the names on the tombstones obliterated, the friends and relatives of the deceased themselves long gone. It is odd that Jack, with his fear of death, would visit such a place, let alone find some ambiguous sense of peace there.

Ernest Becker's 1973 study *The Denial of Death*, one of the few works DeLillo admits as an influence in his fiction, argues that the fear of death and its subsequent repression, the societal failure to accept and normalize death, is the major force in the workings and development of our culture. Tom LeClair has argued that "DeLillo seems to accept Becker's Existential and Rankian positions that the fear of death is the mainspring of human motivation and that man needs to belong to a system of ideas in which mystery exists. But DeLillo differs with Becker's conclusions that repression of the death fear is necessary to live and that 'the problem of heroics is the central one of human life,' for repression and heroic attempts to overcome death place Gladney in life-threatening situations" (LeClair, 1987: p. 213; see also Cowart, 2002: pp. 77–78).

Leonard Wilcox, however, draws attention to the coincidence of DeLillo's postmodern presentation of death, and that described by the French philosopher Jean Baudrillard. For Baudrillard and De-Lillo, "death is the ultimate signified. The single natural event which ultimately cannot be subsumed into simulacra, models, and codes. As Baudrillard conjectures in *Symbolic Exchange and Death*, 'Perhaps only death, the reversibility of death is of a higher order than the code. Only symbolic disorder can breach the code'. . . . And for both Baudrillard and DeLillo the symbolic mediations of contemporary society deprive the individual of an intimate relation with death, with the result that society is haunted by the fear of mortality . . ." (Wilcox, 1991: p. 353, n. 4).

The question that hangs unanswered between Jack and Babette is, "Who will die first?" They have discussed everything openly except for their fear of death (WN, pp. 15, 29–30). This is not the occasional fear of death that anyone might have, that keeps people from reckless acts or exposure to danger, or that might occur when learning of someone else's illness or death. Instead, for Jack and Babette, it is a constant, daily, underlying aspect of their lives. Jack is often startled in the middle of the night by what he identifies as "the more or less normal muscular contraction known as the myoclonic jerk. Is this what it's like, abrupt, peremptory? Shouldn't death, I thought, be a swan dive, graceful, white-winged and smooth, leaving the surface undisturbed?" (WN, p. 18). He looks beyond biology for signs of death, and responds superstitiously: "I awoke in the grip of a death sweat. Defenseless against my own racking fears. . . . The digital reading on the clock-radio was 3:51. . . . What does it mean? Is death odd-numbered? Are there life-enhancing numbers, other numbers charged with menace?" (WN, p. 47). When Jack sees a shadowy figure outside his house, he thinks at once it is the Angel of Death, rather than his father-in-law, Vern Dickey (WN, pp. 232–33). The depth of Babette's fears are not revealed until the mysteries about Dylar are unraveled late in the novel (WN, pp. 184–90). When Jack reports the arrival of the complacent parents with their station wagons bringing the students for a new academic year at College-on-the-Hill, their heaps of consumer goods and their children bearing junk foods and electronic gear to the dorms, Babette says, "I have trouble imagining death at that income level," and Jack responds, "Maybe there is no death as we know it. Just documents changing hands" (WN, p. 6).

Babette counters the fear of death through denial of the dangers of the world as reported on the news; she will not accept that the daily reports about toxic spills, pollution, or disasters hold any significance. The fact that such things occur daily means they can be ignored, they are not serious. As far as what she can do to preserve her health, she dresses in a sweatsuit and runs up the steps of the stadium, she fills her cart in the supermarket with healthy, life-preserving foods such as yogurt, though she does not eat these foods, and she reads the tabloid newspapers, taking in their hopeful accounts of miracle cures and life-after-death, cancer remedies from helpful aliens, and high-tech drugs. Through the tabloids she learns of the experimental drug Dylar, specifically created to remove the fear of death. She is so desperately oppressed by these fears that she volunteers for the discontinued, discredited experiments meeting a scientist in a motel and having sex in exchange for the clandestine treatments.

Jack has several ways of displacing his fears of death. Most importantly, he has attached himself to the most horrible agent of death through the development of his Hitler Studies program. David Cowart notes, "As the physician introduces a discreet quanta of some weakened pathogen into his body to stimulate its immune system, so will Jack, in a professional embrace of the chief death merchant of his age, promote his own resistance to *timor mortis*" (Cowart, 2002: p. 79). He has further insulated himself by the creation of his powerful and enlarged on-campus persona of J. A. K. Gladney in his black academic robe, with his three initials, his physical bulk, and his dark glasses. Jack can restore his spirits after his fear of death has been activated through shopping, through large expenditures and consumption.

He also protects himself from death through the constant repetition of mediated images of death through disaster footage, the clichéd accounts of serial killers and assassins, and the Holocaust (though his Hitler course is designed with the idea of avoiding the death camps and mass killings, focusing instead on crowds, propa-

ganda, Nazi spectacle and uniforms, and other forms of mass per-
suasion). Eugene Goodheart has commented that the "apocalypse
may be the dominant media trope of our time: its endless replay has
inured us to the real suffering it may entail. We repeatedly witness
the assassination of Kennedy, the mushroom cloud over Hiroshima,
the disintegration of the Challenger space shuttle in the sky. Repetition wears away the pain. It also perfects the image of our experienc-
ing it. By isolating the event and repeating it, its content, its horror
evaporates. What we have before us is its form and rhythm. The
event becomes aesthetic and the effect upon us anaesthetic. The
phenomenon is sometimes called kitsch" (Goodheart, p. 122).
Goodheart takes from the Holocaust historian Saul Friedländer a
phrase that suits the repetitive imagery of Nazi rallies, documenta-
ries of wars, assassinations, and disasters: it is the "Kitsch of Death."
Goodheart notes, "Friedländer characterizes it as a 'juxtaposition of
the kitsch aesthetic and of the themes of death that creates the
surprise, that special frisson.' By death, Friedländer means violent,
catastrophic death. But kitsch and death, it would seem, are incom-
patible. How then does one achieve 'the Kitsch of death'? Maybe by
aestheticizing it through apocalyptic lyricism . . ." (Goodheart, p.
123). This "apocalyptic lyricism" is one of the most apparent elements of DeLillo's novels; on the level of sentences and paragraphs,
the phrasing is often beautiful, exuberant, filled both with concise
and apt imagery, rhythmically charged, tonally accurate, using tech-
nical jargon or tabloid clichés as cultural shorthand. On the event-
level, he is portraying assassination, genocide, toxic waste, ecological
disasters, fascism, commodification, and other grave ills.

Jack thinks about the deaths that occur in town, such as that of
old Gladys Treadwell, following her traumatic wanderings in the
mall. He reads the obituaries every morning, noting the ages of those
who died and comparing them to his own age and how many years
they had compared to his present age, and how he would feel about

dying at their ages. How did Genghis Khan feel about his lifespan? Was he ready for death? Then Jack returns to the repeated debate with Babette over who will die first: "I tell her I want to die first. . . . She claims my death would leave a bigger hole in her life than her death would leave in mine . . ." (WN, pp. 99–101). But secretly he knows that he doesn't want to die first; that he is more fearful of death than Babette is. A sharp contrast is provided by Winnie Richards, the university neuroscientist who analyzes the Dylar, and who follows the tradition of Walt Whitman's "Out of the Cradle Endlessly Rocking" and Wallace Stevens' "Sunday Morning." She warns Jack that "it's a mistake to lose one's sense of death, even one's fear of death. Isn't death the boundary we need? Doesn't it give a precious texture to life, a sense of definition? You have to ask whether anything you do in this life would have beauty and meaning without the knowledge you carry of a final line, a border or limit" (WN, p. 217).

But when Jack has been exposed to the cloud of Nyodene D, he can no longer hide from death. He speaks to the SIMUVAC technician after his exposure: "Am I going to die?" "Not as such. . . . Death has entered. It is inside you. You are said to be dying and yet are separate from the dying. . . . It is when death is rendered graphically, is televised so to speak, that you sense an eerie separation between your condition and yourself. . . . A network of symbols has been introduced, an entire awesome technology wrested from the gods. It makes you feel like a stranger in your own dying. I wanted my academic gown and dark glasses" (WN, pp. 136, 137).

Jack's colleague Murray Siskind recognizes the ubiquity of death in the culture, but also the drive to deny it. Speaking with Jack in the supermarket, Murray notes, "Tibetans try to see death for what it is. It is the end of attachment to things. . . . But once we stop denying death, we can proceed calmly to die and then go on to experience uterine rebirth or Judeo-Christian afterlife or out-of-body experience or a trip on a UFO or whatever we wish to call it. . . . Dying is an art in Tibet. . . . Here we don't die, we shop. But the difference is less marked than you think. . . . In cities no one notices specific dying. Dying is a quality of the air." (WN, p. 38). Although Jack turns to Murray for advice after the exposure to Nyodene, Murray is flippant, first treating Jack's heartfelt statement of his fear of dying as a pop-culture allusion, like those that make up the everyday discourse of the faculty members in American Environments. Jack says, "I want to live," and Murray replies, "From the Robert Wise film of the same name, with Susan Hayward as Barbara Graham, a convicted murderess. Aggressive jazz score by Johnny Mandel." (WN, p. 270). Murray offers Jack many ways he can respond to the idea of death planted in his body, but the plenitude of choices which are all equally acceptable, helpful, or not-helpful (another form of white noise), recommended with equal sincerity or insincerity but all apparently bogus. Jack could get around his fear of death by putting his faith in technology, or by concentrating on a life beyond.

"Read up on reincarnation, transmigration, hyperspace, the resurrection of the dead and so on. Some gorgeous systems have evolved from those beliefs. Study them."

"Do you believe in any of these things?"

"Millions of people have believed for thousands of years. Throw in with them. Belief in a second birth, a second life, is practically universal. This must mean something."

"But those gorgeous systems are all so different."

"Pick one you like." (WN, pp. 272–73)

Early in the novel, death is connected to plot and to all manner of plotting. Jack, in his J. A. K. Gladney persona, in his dark glasses and academic gown, has entered into a dialogue in Murray Siskind's Elvis class, helping his friend immeasurably by sharing the weight and seriousness of his charismatic icon Hitler with Murray's far more frivolous (if not lightweight) entertainment icon Elvis. He concludes his comments implying parallels between Hitler and Elvis with a statement he himself does not understand. "'All plots tend to move deathward. This is the nature of plots. Political plots, terrorist plots, lovers' plots, narrative plots, plots that are part of children's games. We edge nearer death every time we plot. It is like a contract that all must sign, the plotters as well as those who are the targets of the plot. Is this true? Why did I say it? What does it mean?'" (WN, p. 26). In DeLillo's *Libra*, published three years after *White Noise*, Win Everett thinks in a similar manner: "Plots carry their own logic. There is a tendency of plots to move towards death. He believed that the idea of death is woven into the nature of every plot. A narrative plot no less than a conspiracy of armed men. The tighter the plot of a story, the more likely it will come to death. A plot in fiction, he believed, is the way we localize the force of death outside the book, play it off, contain it" (DeLillo, *Libra*, p. 221). For someone who wants to avoid thinking of death, this is an unpleasant realization. In his 1936 essay "The Storyteller," Walter Benjamin writes, "Death is the sanction for everything that the storyteller can tell."

Today people live in rooms that have never been touched by death, dry dwellers of eternity, and when their end approaches they are stowed away in sanatoria or hospitals by their heirs. It is, however, characteristic that not only a man's knowledge or wisdom, but above all his real life—and this is the stuff that stories are made of—first assumes transmissable form at the moment of his death. Just as a sequence of images is set in motion inside a man as his life comes to an end—unfolding the views of himself under which he has encountered himself without being aware of it—suddenly in his expressions and looks the unforgettable emerges and imparts to everything that concerned him that authority which even the poorest wretch in dying possesses for the living around him. This authority is at the very source of the story. (Benjamin, 1968: p. 94).

This position, connecting death and plot, especially the resolution of the plot and the end-structure of the narrative, is repeated by narrative theorists and philosophers throughout the twentieth century (Vladimir Propp, Jean-Paul Sartre, Frank Kermode, Claude Bremond, and so on). In *Reading for the Plot*, Peter Brooks traces this history and suggests that "we would do best to speak of the *anticipation of retrospection* as our chief tool in making sense of narrative, the master trope of its strange logic. We have no doubt forgone eternal narrative ends. . . yet still we read in a spirit of confidence, that what remains to be read will restructure the provisional meanings of the already read" (Brooks 1984: p. 23). But the approaching and anticipated resolution is the death of the narrative. Perhaps this is why most of the questions and plot elements remain unresolved at the end. Arthur Salzman argues that "DeLillo's refusal to tie up the numerous loose ends of his narrative (the result of Jack's diagnosis, whether Murray gets approval for his Elvis Studies center, and so on) actually helps to keep *White Noise* from the inevitable death-ward progress to which, so it is rumored in the novel, all plots tend" (Saltzman, 1994: p. 824, n. 10).

Most of the novel is certainly episodic rather than tightly plotted. The reader looking for the plot lines and anticipating the resolution would be placing the elements for the killing of Willy Mink together. Murray presents Jack, with his desperate fear of death and his feeling that death has entered his body, with a "theoretical" way out. "I believe, Jack, there are two kinds of people in the world. Killers and diers. Most of us are diers. . . . It's a way of controlling death. . . . Be the killer for a change. Let someone else be the dier. Let him replace you, theoretically, in that role. You can't die if he does. He dies, you live" (WN, p. 277). "To plot is to live. . . . To plot is to affirm life, to seek shape and control" (WN, p. 278). While this does not seem logical, it is presented as a theory, an idea to try out in the face of unpleasant reality, and since Jack is an intellectual, a new theoretical alternative sounds attractive. It flies directly against his own original conviction that "all plots tend to move deathward," but a life-affirming plot, a way of mastering death (now that Jack has learned that Hitler Studies and dark glasses are insufficient protections) seems inescapable. John Duvall notes that "Murray's theory of killing for life-credit substitutes for Jack's now untenable sense of shopping for existential credit" (Duvall, 1994: p. 143).

All of the traditional elements are in place: Jack has found out about Babette meeting a man in a motel for sex in exchange for obtaining Dylar, so he is the offended husband seeking revenge. There is a surprise visit from his father-in-law, Vernon Dickey, who gives Jack a gun and tells him he will need to use it. While trying to locate Willy Mink, Jack sits in his office with the pistol, bringing it to class: "The gun created a second reality for me to inhabit" (WN, p. 283). The magical weapon of vengeance that will restore him to life by making him a killer instead of a dier, is a Zumwalt automatic, and he feels powerful just to have it with him, unknown to the students and his colleagues. The pistol is even of German origin, tying in with his attempts to attach to himself the power of the Nazis, such as when he named his son Heinrich Gerhardt. Jack plots out the murder of Willy Mink, planning everything as if he is writing a *film noir* script. But then the plot doesn't work out; though he shoots Willy Mink and is excited and seems to be the enthusiastic spectator at the playing out of his script, Jack is shocked when the Dylar and television-addicted Willy Mink shoots Jack in the wrist. Then, suddenly torn from his plot and his killer-character, Jack rescues Willy Mink, clearing his mouth and throat from the Dylar fragments, carrying him to the car he has stolen from his neighbors and taking him to the hospital in Iron City and the German nuns who do not ask questions. He drives back to Blacksmith and returns the bloody stolen car (WN, pp. 290–99).

But everything is left up in the air and there do not seem to be consequences, or even, in plot terms, causes-and-effects. We don't know what happens to Willy Mink, though Jack did not succeed in killing him that night. We do not know what happens to Jack as far as the exposure to Nyodene D, and we see little of the consequences for the Gladney marriage after this year of addiction to Dylar, the sex-for-drugs arrangement Babette made, the violent plans Jack made as he attempted to overpower death, or even if anyone questioned him about the bloody stolen car. The novel ends, as it begins, with products, marketing, and consumption, and the disorder and uneasiness is not because of a toxic cloud, adultery, violence, or the fear of death, but because all of the products have been rearranged in the supermarket.

Commodities, commercial, consumerism, waste

White Noise begins with a leisurely catalogue, a Homeric listing, of items the students bring with them to the dormitories of this expensive, liberal arts college at the start of the academic year, and the description of the well-to-do parents (and with its sham curriculum and unscholarly faculty, as exemplified by the American Environments program and Jack's creation and handling of Hitler Studies). "The parents stand sun-dazed near their automobiles, seeing images of themselves in every direction. . . . They feel a sense of renewal, of communal recognition. . . . something about them suggesting massive insurance coverage. The assembly of station wagons . . . tells the parents they are a collection of the like-minded and the spiritually akin, a people, a nation" (*WN*, pp. 3–4). The accumulation of possessions and the way these establish one's sense of well-being and identity appears throughout the novel.

At the same time, the possessions families accumulate over years, especially through numerous divorces and marriages, of different sets and combinations of parents and children, of children at various ages, moving in and moving out again, becomes a special burden. Jack notes that he and Babette think of the kitchen and bedroom as functional spaces and "we regard the rest of the house as storage space for furniture, toys, all the unused objects of earlier marriages and different sets of children, the gifts of lost in-laws, the hand-me-downs and rummages. Things, boxes. Why do these possessions carry such a sorrowful weight?" (WN, p. 6). There is, in every middle-class household, an inward flow of goods from the abundantly stocked and brightly-lit malls and supermarkets and then an outward flow of crumpled packaging, debris, waste, and, in DeLillo's work, these movements of accumulation and waste mirror psychic stages of well-being and self-regard. Jack is constantly documenting this with his cataloging of the family's consumption, such as when they make lunch (simultaneously but separately), covering the surfaces of the kitchen with discarded packaging and leftover food (WN, p. 7).

Initially, Jack's joy in possession and consumerism is part of his self-inflation, just like his weight, Babette's bulk, his dark glasses and academic gown, his persona as the founder of an academic field, his connection with a terrifying iconic figure. By contrast, Jack watches Murray in the supermarket, picking up items from the Gladney cart and sniffing them, and only purchasing the generic items, white cans and plastic bags. Jack then measures Murray's one light bag against the "mass and variety of our purchases. . . in the sense of replenishment we felt, the sense of well-being, the security and contentment these products bring. . .—it seemed we had achieved a fullness of being that is not known to people who need less, expect less" (WN, pp. 18–20). Jack takes great pleasure in the plenitude of the hardware store and its odd items. But this mood is destroyed by the encounter with Jack's colleague, surprised to see Jack off-campus, who comments that without Jack's academic robe and dark glasses he looks like "a big, harmless, aging, indistinct sort of guy."

Jack's reaction to this is to go on a shopping spree at the mall, urged on by his family: "My family gloried in the event. I was one of them, shopping at last" (*WN*, pp. 82–84). He must become enlarged once more by consuming, by being the giver of largesse and the benefactor to his family.

This notion of accumulation has long been a motif in DeLillo's work. In his analysis of *End Zone,* Mark Osteen notes the connections DeLillo makes between obesity and consumerism, or the ways countries accumulate nuclear weapons arsenals not for use but "merely to *possess* them as symbols of power" (Osteen, 2000; pp. 42–43, also pp. 170–73 on packaging, shopping, the supermarket and mall, how spending causes Jack to grow). Similarly, the weight Jack added when he became J.A.K. Gladney, the literal addition of scholarly, professional *gravitas,* is comforting to Jack and intimidating to others. Jack wants Babette to retain her bulkiness because it is the insulation against death, the bodily equivalent of the bags of goods that fill the Gladney shopping cart or the actions of the giddy shopping spree at the mall. Mark Conroy persuasively argues that, "If the materialism in DeLillo's universe can be given a spiritual inflection, then, it would be a certain Manicheanism: one where spiritual status is marked off by association with the right food and clothing, or proximity to holy ones. . . . Gladney's frantic accretion of weight, wives, and consumer items comes increasingly to be seen as symptomatic of his fear of death, his desire for a talisman to ward it off. . . . the products of modern technology become themselves fetish objects: the miracle drugs, the Promethean airplanes, the electronic temple of modern media" (Conroy, 1994: p. 108).

The other side of the equation, waste, gains in importance in the novel, especially after Jack is convinced that death has entered him with the exposure to Nyodene. Periodically, then, like the Tibetans Murray has described to him, Jack attempts to rid himself of possessions. Jack sees his German tutor Howard Dunlop's copy of *Das*

Aegyptische Todtenbuch, The Egyptian Book of the Dead, and then starts throwing things away, cataloging the things he is discarding (WN, pp. 210–11, again on pp. 249–50). Suddenly more weighed down, rather than built up, by the accumulation of possessions, he catalogues the detritus of life the same way he earlier triumphantly listed the goods, as positive psychic material. As Mark Osteen observes, "If earlier in the novel Jack accumulated commodities to shield him from death, now he throws objects away as if demonically possessed. But the same motive lies behind each valence of this psychic economy: both accumulation and attrition are meant to clear his system, muffle his dread, anesthetize his pain" (Osteen, 2000: p. 183). The cataloging of waste in the later sections of the novel parallels the cataloging in the earlier part of the book of accumulated possessions. Jack goes through the compacted garbage looking for the Dylar Babette had discarded.

I picked through it item by item, mass by shapeless mass, wondering why I felt guilty, a violator of privacy, uncovering intimate and perhaps shameful secrets. It was hard not to be distracted by some of the things they'd chosen to submit to the Juggernaut appliance. But why did I feel like a household spy? Is garbage so private? Does it glow at the core with a personal heat, with signs of one's deepest nature, clues to secret yearning, humiliating flaws? What habits, fetishes, addictions, inclinations? What solitary acts, behavioral ruts? (WN, pp. 246–47)

The family garbage is shameful and fascinating, and Jack reads it as he earlier read the mall and the supermarket. Jack has the detachment of the cultural semiotician, like Murray Siskind: "I found a banana skin with a tampon inside. Was this the dark underside of consumer consciousness?" (See Cowart, 2002: pp. 74–76 for discussion of the items in the Gladney household garbage recapitulating themes and motifs from all of DeLillo's novels.) Later Jack lists the garbage and debris in the car of the Stovers, the car he uses in his plan to kill Willy Mink (WN, p. 288). Tom LeClair has argued that the form and style of the novel itself recapitulates the thematic use of waste: "In its list-like style, discontinuities, and repetition, its jammed subgenres and intellectual foolishness, *White Noise* is . . . a novelistic heap of waste. . . . Like the other systems novelists, DeLillo recycles American waste into art to warn against entropy, both thermodynamic and informational" (LeClair, 1987: p. 212).

In DeLillo's *End Zone*, Gary Harkness walks out into the desert and encounters a pile of excrement, and this is an epiphany for him, an existential moment in which he feels terrified by the "one thing which did not betray its definition. . . . There was the graven art of a curse in that sight. It was overwhelming, a terminal act. . . . I thought of men embedded in the ground, all killed, billions, flesh cauterized into the earth, bits of bone and hair and nails, a man-planet, a fresh intelligence revolving through the system" (*End Zone* pp. 69–70). More recently, in *Underworld*, Nick Shay is an entrepreneur of waste recycling and he is entirely obsessed with the garbage and all forms of human detritus. For him, the recycling of human garbage is an act of beauty that could only be described in the language associated with the sacred. Nick watches the operations in the vast recycling shed with his six-year-old granddaughter, Sunny.

The tin, the paper, the plastics, the styrofoam. It all flies down the conveyor belts, four hundred tons a day, assembly lines of garbage, sorted, compressed and baled, transformed in the end to square-edged units, products again, wire-bound and smartly stacked and ready to be marketed. Sunny loves this place and so do the other kids who come with their parents or teachers to stand on the catwalk and visit the exhibitions. Brightness streams from skylights down to the floor of the shed, falling on the tall machines with a numinous glow. Maybe we feel a reverence for waste, for the redemptive qualities of the things we use and discard. (*Underworld*, p. 809)

Shay's assistant Brian Classic visits the Fresh Kills landfill on Staten Island and is awestruck by the management of the fifty million tons of waste there, "and he saw himself for the first time as a member of an esoteric order, they were adepts and seers, crafting the future, the city planners, the waste managers, the compost technicians, the landscapers who would build a hanging gardens here, a park one day out of every kind of used and lost and eroded object of desire" (*Underworld*, p. 185).

Advertising, marketing, brand names, packaging, and other promotions of consumerism; all of those arts that instill desire for possession and accumulation have also been part of DeLillo's novels since the beginning of his writing career (started, after all, once he left advertising). As Mark Osteen has pointed out about advertising executive Clinton Bell in DeLillo's first novel, *Americana*: "Clinton conceives of his family as ad images mirroring those in his basement archive of videotaped TV commercials, which he reruns repeatedly to 'find the common threads and nuances' in those that have achieved 'high test ratings' (A, p. 84). These mass-cultural artifacts, replacing the personal mementos and home movies preserved by other middle-class males, are his Americana . . ." (Osteen, 2000: p. 19). In *Underworld* there is the advertising man Wainwright "who will indiscriminately market anything from gasoline to toxic gas, for whom nuclear weapons are just another image for selling products. . . . Wainwright's greatest professional pride is the Minute Maid orange juice campaign, which made bright orange cans 'orgasmically visual' to millions of (mostly female) consumers. By tapping into undercurrents of desire, Wainwright 'connects millions of people across a continental landmass, compelling them to buy a certain product' (U, pp. 533–34)" (Osteen, 2000: p. 241).

In DeLillo's earlier novels, characters realize that they have become commodities themselves, and they struggle to escape this. Rock star Bucky Wunderblick in *Great Jones Street* tries to separate himself from the rock star lifestyle, to change his image and his music, to go into hiding, but everything is seen as some other marketing tack. The reclusive writer Bill Gray in *Mao II* has become a brand name to be found on the shelves of any bookstore. Similarly, the Gladney household is permeated with advertising slogans and brand-names. Jack listens to Steffie mumbling in her sleep the words "*Toyota Celica*" and this strikes him "with the impact of a moment of splendid transcendence" (WN, pp. 148–49).

White noise

The white noise of the title appears, appropriately, throughout the novel, not spiking to attention or disappearing, but always a sort of low hum in the background to whatever is happening in the novel; there is no escape. It is one of the speculations about what death is (WN, p. 189), and it is the nighttime traffic sound that washes over the Gladneys in their bedrooms (WN, pp. 4, 29). There are the various emergency alarms that the Gladneys hear and identify, but which cause no response: "The smoke alarm went off in the hallway upstairs, either to let us know the battery had just died or because the house was on fire. We finished our lunch in silence" (WN, p. 8); later they ignore the air raid sirens and fire trucks making loudspeaker announcements about the airborne toxic event (WN, pp. 115–16).

It is the sound of household machinery such as washing machine, trash compactor, dish washer, or refrigerator. There are bits of overheard telephone conversations: "Heinrich said to someone on the phone, 'Animals commit incest all the time. So how unnatural can it be?'" or "Neutrinos go right through the earth" (WN, p. 34). There are rumors during the different emergencies in Blacksmith: "Remarks existed in a state of permanent flotation. No one thing was more or less plausible than any other thing" (WN, p. 125).

The television and radios are always on in the house, sounds coming from various rooms, each set showing something else: an advertisement, an exercise show, disaster footage. These disembodied voices appear as separate sentences, free-floating units that enter into everyone's mind indiscriminately: "I heard the TV say: 'Let's sit half lotus and think about our spines'" (WN, p. 18). "Someone turned on the TV set at the end of the hall, and a woman's voice said, 'If it breaks easily into pieces, it is called shale. When wet it smells like clay'" (WN, pp. 28–29). "The TV said: 'Now we will put the little feelers on the butterfly'" (WN, p. 96). "In the four-hundred-thousand-dollar Nabisco Dinah Shore" (WN, p. 228). "The voice upstairs said: 'Now watch this. Joanie is trying to snap Ralph's patella with a *bushido* stun kick. She makes contact, he crumples, she runs'" (WN, p. 245). Dylar-addicted Willy Mink has phrases he has picked up from television dizzily interspersed in his own dialogue (WN, pp. 294, 295, 299).

Even more multi-layered than the home is the white noise of the centers of commerce. In the supermarket, Jack realizes "the place was awash with noise. The toneless systems, the jangle and skid of carts, the loudspeaker and coffee-making machines, the cries of children. And over it all, or under it all, a dull and unlocatable roar, as of some form of swarming life just outside the range of human apprehension" (WN, p. 36). During the family's wild shopping excursion in the mall, "A band played live Muzak. Voices rose ten stories from the gardens and promenades, a roar that echoed and swirled through the vast gallery, mixing with noises from the tiers, with shuffling feet and chiming bells, the hum of escalators, the sound of people eating, the human buzz of some vivid and happy transaction" (WN, p. 84).

Perhaps the most arresting representations of the white noise are the repeated phrases in series of threes: three hotel names (WN, p. 15), three credit card companies (WN, p. 99), three brands of mints

(WN, p. 218), three medicines (WN, p. 276), and "Random Access Memory, Acquired Immune Deficiency Syndrome, Mutual Assured Destruction" (WN, p. 289). These are not attributed to any over-heard sources like the television but just appear periodically through the book, as part of Jack's first-person narration, though not as part of his thinking, and he does not comment on them. Jack does not reject the white noise from whatever source, and he does not provide interpretations or reflections upon it; the unmediated placement of the sentences and phrases makes the inclusion more complex for the reader, as well as being formally mimetic of the situation of the characters. He responds with joyful transcendence to his daughter whispering a car name in her sleep, though it will be left to Murray to relish the bombardment of bits of information, to interpret the particles and waves. The only place of silence in the entire novel, as Jack stands and listens, The Old Burying Ground of Blacksmith Village (WN, p. 96), out on the road, pre-twentieth century, forgotten, lost to the world, out of the loop, both comforting and disturbing.

American Environments

One of the genres of *White Noise* would be the "university novel," established first through British writers Kingsley Amis' *Lucky Jim* (1954); Malcolm Bradbury's *Eating People Is Wrong* (1959), *Stepping Westward* (1965), *The History Man* (1975), and *Rates of Exchange* (1986); and David Lodge's *Changing Places* (1975), and *Small World* (1984), and carried into recent American fiction by such works as Robert Grudin's *Book* (1992) and Richard Russo's *Straight Man* (1997). (Mention should also be made of Vladimir Nabokov's *Pale Fire* [1962], though this work, like *White Noise*, transcends the generic boundaries of the university novel.) These novels are genial satires, more humorous or hilarious depending upon one's knowledge of the hidden workings of universities in general, and English or History departments in particular. They tend to provide caricatures of the eccentric and obsessed professors, some of the esoteric research and complex bureaucracies, university and departmental politics, jargon, and current intellectual fashions, and the curriculum.

To some extent, this description fits *White Noise* perfectly, though it is only a small portion of the novel. The chancellor of College-on-the-Hill encouraged Jack to change his appearance towards the dark, heavy, and fearful, to become J.A.K. Gladney for the added *gravitas*, and to create his own marketing niche of Hitler Studies. We see little of Jack's colleagues at the college (just the neuroscientist Winnie Richards who must be found racing through the woods on campus, and who only enters the book when Jack seeks information about Dylar and its creator), the college administrators, or the students, who appear primarily as an audience for Jack's comments on Hitler, Elvis, and death. This narrowness of focus would seem to take *White Noise* away from the satiric genre of the university novel, except for the scenes involving the American Environments faculty.

In just a handful of pages, DeLillo's brilliant mockery of the academic American environment, both Jack Gladney's charlatan approach and the professoriate, represented by the American Environments program, chaired by Alfonse (Fast Food) Stompanato, captures many elements of the post-1970s university (Conroy, 1994: pp. 101–2; see also Duvall, 1994: p. 138; and Reeve and Kerridge, 1994: pp. 306–7, 310). "The teaching staff is composed almost solely of New York emigrés; smart, thuggish, movie-mad, trivia-crazed. They are here to decipher the natural language of the culture, to make a formal method of the shiny pleasures they'd known in their Europe-shadowed childhoods" (WN, p. 9). Murray Siskind, "a visiting lecturer on living icons" (WN, p. 10), describes the internal politics of the department, worried that the territorial rights of Dimitrios

Cotsakis, "a three-hundred-pound former rock 'n' roll bodyguard," will prevent him from starting an Elvis Studies program, modeled on Jack's Hitler Studies; Cotsakis is later removed from being Murray's rival when he is lost in the surf off Malibu (*WN*, p. 160). During wild lunch scenes, including food fights, the faculty members constantly test each other on their experiences in the lower strata of American life and attachment to, or knowledge of, popular culture: "Did you ever brush your teeth with your finger?" or "Where were you when James Dean died?" (*WN*, pp. 64–69). Mark Osteen, discussing the reaction of Wilder to television, notes that Wilder's "transient attention makes him the perfect target for advertisements. Such childlike behavior prolonged into adulthood yields the frivolities of the 'American Environments' faculty, who turn memories into prepackaged responses. . . . an 'essentially childish' culture in which most activities have become elaborate forms of play and in which adults are encouraged to indulge in nostalgic self-gratification" (Osteen, 2000: p. 175). In addition to his Elvis seminar, Murray develops a Cinema of Car Crashes Course (*WN*, pp. 204–8).

Murray, who at least knows the *Tibetan Book of the Dead* and reads magazines, is surprised to discover that his colleagues in the program do not read anything more than cereal boxes, and the focus is on nostalgia and personal experience. He is a cultural semiotician; he reads everything around him in terms of signs and sign systems. There is nothing that is insignificant, and he takes pleasure in reading this new environment in the small-town, in the middle of the country, removed from the media and cultural centers, but filled with new experiences for him. He enjoys watching the Gladney children in their interactions and television viewing; he feels raptures over diagonal parking in the main street of a small town, generic packaging of products in the supermarket, UFOs and tabloid news. He often analyzes the phenomena of Blacksmith, and especially Jack, in ways that seem persuasive and sensible, as when Murray explains how Jack has used Hitler to protect himself from death, or that Jack feels so good when he is with Wilder because Wilder doesn't have the anticipation and fear of death (WN, p. 274, 276). He can analyze his own role in the novel and the rooming house as fulfilling a stereotypical, motifemic slot as "the Jew." Thomas Peyser argues that "Murray's cultural position as a cosmopolitan, Jewish intellectual may have much to do with his ability to turn a loftily critical eye on American custom. He could almost serve as the walking embodiment of Thorstein Veblen's essay, 'The Intellectual Preeminence of Jews in Modern Europe.' His position as the quasi-outsider, as the stranger, allows for his magisterial penetration of the culture . . ." (Peyser, 1996: p. 263).

As the newest faculty member in American Environments, Murray often seems unsure of himself in the lunchtime competitions. Even in his Elvis seminar, Murray is in the position of imitating Jack and his success with Hitler Studies; his insecurity and gratitude towards Jack for visiting the Elvis class, sharing Hitler and lifting Elvis' stature, is transparent. Jack makes a series of parallels between Hitler and Elvis, and discusses the crowds for both (WN, pp. 70–74). Jack watches Murray and thinks, "His eyes showed a deep gratitude. I had been generous with the power and madness at my disposal, allowing my subject to be associated with an infinitely lesser figure, a fellow who sat in La-Z-Boy chairs and shot out TVs" (WN, p. 73). But off-campus, Murray seems the master theorist and teacher, and Jack is the ephebe. This is first apparent in the visit to the "Most Photographed Barn in America."

Murray explains, "Being here is a kind of spiritual surrender. We see only what the others see. The thousands who were here in the past, those who will come in the future. We've agreed to be part of a collective perception. . . . We can't get outside the aura. We're part of the aura" (WN, pp. 12–13). People take packed tour buses out to photograph "The Most Photographed Barn in America" simply because it is announced and advertised as "The Most Photographed Barn in America"; the advertisement makes it the most photographed barn because people want to participate in the phenomenon. They want to be photographed taking pictures of the barn and of the other photographers. The barn cannot be seen as a building any more, but only as "The Most Photographed Barn in America." Numerous critics have discussed Walter Benjamin's key essay "The Work of Art in the Age of Mechanical Reproduction" in connection with "The Most Photographed Barn in America." "John Frow quite rightly points out that Benjamin's hope that mechanical reproduction would destroy the pseudo-religious aura of cultural artifacts has been subverted and that, instead, 'the commodification of culture has worked to preserve the myth of origins and of authenticity' (Frow, p. 181). Here, as elsewhere in the novel, the myth of authenticity that is aura comes into being through mediation, the intertextual web of prior representations. . . . The most dangerous element of the most photographed barn, finally, is the tourists' collective spiritual surrender precisely because it is a desired surrender" (Duvall, 1994: p. 140; see Cowart's important analysis, with reference to Walker Percy on the Grand Canyon; Cowart, 2002: pp. 86–87; also see Lentricchia's essay in Lentricchia, ed., *WN*, esp. pp. 88–92). The willing collective surrender, and the investing of the ordinary with the devotion of the sacred, of course recalls the sort of phenomenon Jack focuses on in his Hitler Studies program.

Of all the characters in *White Noise*, Murray often displays the awareness of DeLillo himself towards the most mundane, everyday aspects of the culture. Charles Molesworth notes, "No other contemporary novelist could be said to outstrip DeLillo in his ability to depict that larger social environment we blandly call everyday life. Brand names, current events, fads, the society of the spectacle, and the rampant consumerism that has become our most noticeable, if not our most important, contribution to history, are all plentifully and accurately recorded in his work" (Molesworth, 1991: p. 143). In his interview with Anthony DeCurtis, DeLillo said, "In *White Noise* . . . I tried to find a kind of radiance in dailiness. . . . Imagine someone from the third world who has never set foot in a place like that suddenly transported to an A&P in Chagrin Falls, Ohio. Wouldn't he be elated or frightened? Wouldn't he sense that something transcending is about to happen to him in the midst of all this brightness" (DeCurtis, 1991: p. 63). Murray sometimes sounds like the literary critics who have analyzed *White Noise* or DeLillo's other novels.

Despite all of this, Murray is seen by many critics in a harshly negative way. John Duvall considers Murray to be "the true villain of *WN*" (Duvall, 1994: pp. 139–43), while Tom LeClair compares Murray to Mephistopheles for the way he tempts Jack into falling into the violent plotline he suggests "theoretically" of being a killer instead of a dier. For LeClair, Murray is something of a parasite (LeClair, 1987: pp. 220–21). Mark Conroy considers both Murray and Jack to be parasitic (though the same may be said for all of the American Environments faculty: "There is for both Gladney and Siskind an additional source of precious professorial authority: charisma by association. Both are making their careers by attaching themselves, as critics are wont to do, to some eminent figure, whose glory they parasitically procure" (Conroy, 1994: p. 101). Some critics have considered Murray to be as *outré*, as mad, as Dylar-addicted Willy Mink. Linking Murray and Mink, Reeve and Kerridge note that, "Rationality in *WN* is always on the brink of being overwhelmed" (Reeves and Kittredge, 1994: pp. 303–5). John Duvall notes subtle differences between Murray and Mink, with Murray as structuralist or semiotician, and Mink as postmodernist (Duvall, 1994: p. 147).

Hitler and Fascism

What is the role of Hitler in *White Noise?* Hitler appears in DeLillo's other novels, of course, more recognizably perhaps than he does through Jack's Hitler Studies. But DeLillo's Hitler is less the historical figure than the iconic Hitler constructed variously first through the propaganda created during the Nazi era, created and directed by Hitler himself, and, secondly, constructed through the representations of Hitler in film and on television. Hitler is part of the white noise of American culture, on television every night in some way ("He's always on. We couldn't have television without him" [WN, p. 63]). On the one hand, the historical Hitler is the architect of the Holocaust, the most horrific mass-murderer in history, but when treated iconically he is just a dark celebrity, like Marilyn Monroe or James Dean. It is not too farfetched, in this way of thinking, for Hitler to be paired with Elvis Presley for the purposes of Murray's development of his own niche in academe. When Jack selects Hitler for career purposes, as Reeves and Kittredge note, " 'Hitler' has here become a signifier in a code that does not register the moral significance of his name, but trades him as a commodity on the academic market" (Reeve and Kerridge, 1994: p. 307; see also Osteen, 2000: pp. 167–68). Jack's description of his only course, Advanced Nazism, required for all Hitler majors, follows this sensational, emotional presentation of Nazi surface spectacle. According to the course description, the course focuses on crowd scenes, parades, rallies, uniforms, and the continuing mass appeal of fascist tyranny; the film he has put together creates "a scene that resembled a geometric longing, the formal notation of some powerful mass desire. There was no narrative voice. Only chants, songs, arias, speeches, cries, cheers, accusations, shrieks" (WN, pp. 25–26). Jack finds a similar aesthetic sense, rather than a practical sense, in the Nazis themselves, when he explains Albert Speer's plan for building "structures that would decay gloriously, impressively, like Roman ruins" (WN, p. 246). This aestheticization of politics, like Friedländer's notion of the "Kitsch of Death" as the aestheticization of the apocalypse, was decried by Walter Benjamin in his epilogue to "The Work of Art in the Age of Mechanical Reproduction":

Fascism attempts to organize the newly created proletarian masses without affecting the property structure which the masses strive to eliminate. . . . Fascism seeks to give them an expression while preserving property. The logical result of Fascism is the introduction of aesthetics into political life. The violation of the masses, whom Fascism, with its *Führer* cult, forces to their knees, has its counterpart in the violation of an apparatus which is pressed into the production of ritual values. . . . (Benjamin, 1936: p. 241)

Ironically, Jack's attachment to Hitler, who spread death to so many millions, is because of his tremendous fear of death and his feeling of the magical power that emanates from such evil power, and because of his inability to read the kitsch, the media, the crowd manipulation, and so on that is the subject of his course, his film, and the impromptu talk he gives in Murray's Elvis seminar. It is emblematic of his general intellectual disconnection that he doesn't understand his own comments, and he doesn't see through the theoretical dichotomy of killers and diers Murray foments that leads to the shooting of Willy Mink.

John Duvall has also noted Jack's obtuseness while cocooned in his academic area: ". . . each element of Jack's world mirrors back to him a postmodern, decentralized totalitarianism that this professional student of Hitler is unable to read. Jack's failure to recognize proto-fascist urges in an aestheticized American consumer culture is all the more striking since he emphasizes in his course Hitler's manipulation of mass cultural aesthetics (uniforms, parades, rallies). This failure underscores the key differences between Hitler's fascism and American proto-fascism: ideology ceases to be a conscious choice, as it was for the National Socialists, and instead becomes in contemporary America more like the Althusserian notion of ideology as unconscious system of representation" (Duvall, 1994: p. 128). Jack named his son Heinrich Gerhardt in order to give him that power because Jack knew that he himself was weak, hidden behind a façade. When Jack mistakes his father-in-law for the figure of Death he picks up his copy of *Mein Kampf* to ward off death. De-Lillo has said, "The damage caused by Hitler was so enormous that Gladney feels he can disappear inside it and that his own puny dread will be overwhelmed by the vastness, the monstrosity of Hitler himself. He feels that Hitler is not only bigger than life, as we say of famous figures, but bigger than death" (DeCurtis, 1991: p. 63; see also Murray's explanation of this, WN, p. 274).

The magic attaches to elements connected with Hitler, such as fascism and the German language. During the Airborne Toxic Event, Jack drives his car off the paved roads in his attempt to stay close to the right-wing survivalists who he assumes would know what to do in such an emergency, as if they could protect him. Jack's recognition of his weakness and the power he attributes to things German is the reason he has never been able to learn the German language. Jack struggles with German in secret. His fear, as the conference comes closer, is that the other scholars will discover he doesn't know German: "I was living . . . on the edge of a landscape of vast shame" (WN, pp. 31–32, see also p. 165). His fear is so great that he goes off campus to the strange tutor, Howard Dunlop (who has also taught meteorology and yachting), another roomer in Murray's boarding house, even putting up with Dunlop reaching into his mouth to manipulate his tongue. Jack finally creates a speech in German at the Hitler conference, using as many cognates as possible, looking up every word in the German dictionary with the help of his family. He spends the first Hitler Studies conference hiding in his office avoiding the other speakers (WN, p. 261). He finally takes childish delight using his tiny scraps of German with the nun in the hospital, Sister Hermann Marie, after he has shot Willy Mink, pointing out common items in German while the nun dresses his wounded wrist (WN, p. 302).

In an earlier DeLillo novel in which Hitler played an important role, *Running Dog*, this commodification of the dictator was made clear. The main object of desire in the novel is a film purportedly shot in the *Führerbunker* during the last weeks of the Second World War, as the Allies were surrounding Berlin, alleged to show erotic acts perhaps involving Hitler, Eva Braun, or other high Nazi officials and the women who were said to pass through the bunker. According to Lightborne, the shady dealer in pornographic films, "You see, he's endlessly fascinating. The whole Nazi era. People can't get enough. If it's Nazis, it's automatically erotic. The violence, the rituals, the leather, the jackboots. The whole thing for uniforms and paraphernalia" (*Running Dog*, p. 52). When finally revealed, the film is not pornographic, but is Nazi kitsch; Hitler's home movie shows the greatest mass-murderer in history doing a very exact imitation of Charlie Chaplin's parody of Hitler in Chaplin's film, *The Great Dictator*. Hitler is revealed with Chaplin's "sweet, epicene, guilty little smile." As David Cowart points out, "It is the smile of ambiguous identity, any-gendered and replete with knowledge of the infinite fluidity of the self. Portraying the Chaplin who, in *The Great Dictator*, has portrayed *Der Führer* twice over (for the great comic portrays Hitler himself and the little barber who, as the plot unfolds, impersonates Hitler), Hitler subverts and reverses the original satire, characterizing identity as a hall of mirrors, a simulacrum's simulacrum" (Cowart, 2002: pp. 63–64; see also Osteen, 2000: pp. 103–4, 112–16, on these same points, and Keesey, 1993: p. 110; Paul Cantor's essay in Lentricchia, ed., WN, pp. 39–62).

Media and technology

Television, tabloids, radio, film, are ubiquitous in *White Noise*. In the Gladney household, television and radio voices filter through the house as white noise, as the key authorities on every issue, but just heard in short sound-bites as people go from place to place or change channels. "Waves and radiation," he said. "I've come to understand that the medium is a primal force in the American home. Sealed-off, timeless, self-contained, self-referring. It's like a myth being born right there in our living room, like something we know in a dreamlike and preconscious way" (WN, p. 51). It is so difficult to picture someone who is not exposed to television, that Jack recommends Wilder's half-brother Eugene, who lives in the outback with one of Babette's former husbands. Eugene could be a case study for Murray to study because he has been growing up entirely without television, like a feral child, "a savage plucked from the bush, intelligent and literate but deprived of the deeper codes and messages that mark his species as unique" (WN, p. 50). Babette is the only character in the novel who seems to be at all negative about television, the only one who wants to control and diminish it (probably a far smaller number than the general population, or of the hyper-critical university faculty population, who would actually have objections about the impact of television). Her best effort is to try to force the family to have one meal together every Friday night, as a ritual, with takeout Chinese food, and to watch television altogether, instead of each watching television separately. "She seemed to think that if kids watched television one night a week with parents or stepparents, the effect would be to de-glamorize the medium in their eyes, make it wholesome, domestic sport. Its narcotic undertow and eerie diseased brain-sucking power would be gradually reduced" (WN, p. 16).

Most of the time, the family makes fun of Babette's attempts to become thinner and healthier, of her voluntary community teaching in such subjects as standing and walking, in her reading tabloids to Mr. Treadwell, in her outdated knowledge and bits of memorized trivia and formulas. But this changes in the most startling way, with everyone in the family transfixed by the image of Babette appearing on television. This produces in the family tremendous disorientation and strangeness: "We were being shot through with Babette. Her image was projected on our bodies, swam in us and through us. Babette of electrons and photons, of whatever forces produced that gray light we took to be her face. . . . Only Wilder remained calm. . . ." The scene ends with Wilder softly crying and Murray taking notes while the rest of the family at first watches in awe and then they disperse (WN, pp. 102–4). N. Katherine Hayles refers to this as a "reinscription" of Babette into "waves and radiation" when she is shown on television (Hayles, 1990: p. 410). Appearing on television takes on elements of the sacred, of an unworldly, out-of-body, perhaps even afterlife experience. The sound is off but no one goes to turn the volume up; they are observing Babette literally in a new light: "It was her but it wasn't her. . . . The kids were flushed with excitement but I felt a certain disquiet. I tried to tell myself it was only television . . . and not some journey out of life and death, not some mysterious separation" (WN, p. 103).

Although Babette is just showing her class in the church basement the fine points of walking, she seems to be speaking from another realm of the universe ("Was she dead, missing, disembodied? Was this her spirit . . . some two-dimensional facsimile released by the power of technology . . . pausing to say goodbye to us from the fluorescent screen?" [WN, p. 102]). Just as the murderers and assassins long to be captured on film, even evaluate their success or failure not on whether or not they remain free but whether and how they are shown on television; just as the evacuees from the toxic cloud and the passengers from the near-plane crash feel upset primarily with the lack of media coverage, Babette's appearance on the family television seems to make her more than just a familiar human figure. Being on television is somehow a change of status, but it is puzzling to understand what the meaning of the change might be. The others in the family have been left behind by Babette. Jack thinks, "I'd seen her just an hour ago, eating eggs, but her appearance on the screen made me think of her as some distant figure from the past, some ex-wife and absentee mother, a walker in the mists of the dead. If she was not dead, was I?" (*WN*, p. 103). For death-phobic Jack, it is as if the question from the beginning of the book, "Who will die first?," has been answered. But any appearance on television is transformative and elevating, whether it is because one has become a celebrity or is shown being captured by the police after committing a crime. Mark Conroy notes, "Indeed, it is a corollary of the Manichean emphasis upon personhood, upon the physical as a prerequisite for spiritual authority, that the mere fact of one's positioning by the mass media is itself the sign of election. The moral dimension to the publicity—whether it is achieved through mass murder, in the case of Heinrich's pen pal, or through good deeds—becomes secondary to the fact of election itself" (Conroy, 1994: p. 108).

Television has one primary function beyond providing entertainment and giving information and commercials: it validates human activity, it does not merely show things. Events and people must be on television for it to acquire meaning, or even in order to exist. This is especially true for disasters and crimes. Heinrich calls the family to join him when "plane crash footage" is shown, and although Babette desperately searches for wholesome and uplifting television during the Friday night family dinners, she always loses as the rest of the family wants to watch one distant disaster after another, or perhaps the same disaster again and again (*WN*, pp. 63–64). When

Bee reaches the terminal after what seemed like a near crash of the airplane she was on, her first words are not about her relief but, "Where's the media?" Told there is no media in Iron City, she says with exasperation, "They went through all that for nothing?" (*WN*, p. 92). Similarly, the evacuees during the Airborne Toxic Event, listening to their radios and watching battery-powered televisions while huddled under plastic sheets and trying to avoid the toxic plume of Nyodene, are chiefly furious because there's nothing about them on the network news. "The airborne toxic event is a horrifying thing. Our fear is enormous. Even if there hasn't been great loss of life, don't we deserve something for our suffering, our human worry, our terror? Isn't fear news?" (*WN*, p. 155). The biggest failure of Heinrich's rooftop sniper pen pal is not that he killed people, but that he did so in a place without media, and in retrospect, it's not that he wouldn't kill people, but that he would plan to do it where the event would be covered properly.

In American Environments, chair Alfonse Stompanato's analysis of disaster coverage in California is important, compared to places whose disasters go unrecorded (*WN*, p. 66). It is important because it is filled with cameras, television networks, helicopters with cameras covering traffic that could be used for unfolding events (like the slow-speed "chase" of O. J. Simpson's white pickup truck on the California highways, carried live on CNN and every news station in the country), while in places around the world that lack the cameras and technology, that do not have twenty-four hour news, satellite uplinks, and a large paying cable-television audience, far larger events take place constantly (volcanoes, famine, civil wars, assassinations, floods, ferry-sinkings, and so on), but do not get television coverage. It's as if those events did not take place (at least as far as everyone beyond the immediate circle of victims and their families and friends is concerned). California is important because of the technology, and because it has many disasters itself that are minutely covered—from forest fires to storms that cause mudslides and the washing away of multi-million dollar homes to serial killers and school and workplace shootings. California almost fills the entire programming space for disasters.

As with the repeated images of violence and the Holocaust, this overplay on television tends to create an anaesthetizing impact on the audience, more connoisseurs of disaster footage than worried and sympathetic comrades to the victims. Babette's disinterest in disasters and toxic events is a result of the fact that they are everyday events on the news. "How serious can it be if it happens all the time? Isn't the definition of a serious event based on the fact that it's not an everyday occurrence?" (WN, p. 166). The more the images are repeated, the less they are associated with the suffering they depict, and the more they become like other programs, fictional or documentary. Since fictional programs on television imitate the mimetic forms and surfaces of the "real," the "non-fictional," these differences are elided or purposely confused. Sometimes "real" and recognizable television journalists, politicians, etc. appear in fictional films or television programs portraying themselves. Of course, television and other media manipulate and control audiences, creating artificial worlds of consumer demand through their repeated commercial messages and slick images of beauty, desire, and fulfillment (on this point see Keesey, 1993: pp. 138–40).

Jeremy Green, focusing on violence in DeLillo's work, particularly in *Libra*, has discussed the way we are made into the "society of the spectacle," with certain images shown again and again until everyone has seen them, how both Lee Harvey Oswald and the Texas Highway Killer perform "live" murders, captured on film inadvertently and shown repeatedly (see Green, 1999: pp. 584–86, 593–96, also p. 596n.5 on DeLillo's play *Valparaiso* and the television interview). The Zapruder film of the Kennedy assassination and Jack Ruby's on-camera shooting of Lee Harvey Oswald, Sirhan Sirhan's shooting of Robert Kennedy as he was entering the room filled with cheering supporters and many news-cameras, seep into the communal consciousness and self-definition. In DeLillo's *Underworld*, the Texas Highway Killer Gilkey shows how videotaping his crimes and being interviewed on television were to give him existence: "He commits the crimes in order to be on television, which is the only way he exists at all; his murders permit him to assume radiant form and thereby become one with the other viewers" (Osteen, 2000: p. 235).

There is another prominent media form in *White Noise*, besides television and radio: the supermarket tabloid. Babette reads to Mr. Treadwell, "from the *National Enquirer*, the *National Examiner*, the *National Express*, the *Globe*, the *World*, the *Star*. The old fellow demands his weekly dose of cult mysteries" (*WN*, p. 6). Jack's earlier observation of Babette's reading to Mr. Treadwell is emotionally detached; he is merely baffled about the appeal. After the Nyodene exposure, however, Jack listens to Babette reading to Old Man Treadwell and a group of blind people from the tabloid newspapers while they have been evacuated to the countryside. Jack now takes a deep interest in the life-saving, miraculous narratives of the tabloids, the alternative belief systems presented simultaneously and accepted silently by the elderly auditors to Babette's reading (*WN*, pp. 137–41). Tom LeClair has observed that Murray's presentation of the mysteries of the supermarket provides the life that's closest to the tabloid world heavens, miracles, and afterlife stories (LeClair, 1987: pp. 228–29). Television and tabloids appear in *White Noise* as spiritual channels with the voices of the dead, "holy chants that invoke commodities for protection or supplication" (Osteen, 2000: pp. 166–67, 174–76). The tabloids published the numerous stories about the miraculous saving of mankind, sightings of celebrities long thought to be dead, (such as Elvis Presley), cures for deadly illnesses provided by alien cultures, reincarnation, proof of the afterlife, one belief system after another juxtaposed non-judgmentally. In addition, the tabloids published ads for those people suffering from fear of death, people like Babette so desperate to overcome her fear she would have sex with a shady, Dylar-addicted, ostracized scientist in order to be given the pills. The television intermeshed with what was left of Willy Mink's mind so thoroughly that the disembodied voices from television spoke through him.

Technology

One conspicuous change for current, and especially young, readers of *White Noise* (in contrast with the readers at the time of the book's publication in 1985) is the relative lack of computers and the culture of the internet. Though technology is a major element of the novel, except for television it is not part of the Gladney home or even the College-on-the-Hill campus life or faculty field of reference. Certainly Heinrich and the American Environments faculty would be fully engaged with the Internet, Heinrich would be sending e-mails to his imprisoned pen pal (what a quaint term that seems now, "pen pal"), and perhaps Jack would be using software to help him learn German instead of allowing the eccentric autodidact, Howard Dunlop, to grasp and manipulate his tongue into proper pronunciation. Since 1985 was not actually such a long time ago, it may be difficult to recognize what a technological difference there is between then and now.

Computers and technology in *White Noise* were at the cutting edge for 1985, when the home personal computer was just being introduced; its memory and capabilities were miniscule compared to today's computers (and even more miniscule compared to whatever is available whenever you are reading this). Only university science researchers and the military were involved with the internet, and the World Wide Web had not yet been named or publicly released (its name apparently evolved from William Gibson's 1984 novel *Neuromancer*, and it was "invented" in 1990 by the European Particle Physics Laboratory, CERN). As a marker of distance, instead of years, technology serves well: when *White Noise* was published, there were no cell-phones, DVDs, MP3s, HDTVs, and so on.

Within the Gladney home, besides the constant presence of television and radio, telephone calls come in from market-survey companies, with the speaker a computer-generated woman's voice that would ask a series of questions; Steffie answers all of the questions with serious interest (WN, p. 48). There is, as Donald Keesey notes, the information overload pulverizing the consumer into submission, eventually becoming the white noise of the lived-environment (Keesey, 1993: pp. 140–41). Heinrich and the other technologically astute and interested will be the most comfortable citizens of the new technological society and Jack and Babette will be left baffled, always playing catch-up and trying to rely upon their now out-of-date trivia and on their children. According to Tom LeClair, "The knowledge that Heinrich and others impose on Jack and Babette is often specialized, taken out of its scientific context and expressed in its own nomenclature. The 'waves and radiation' are beyond the capability of 'natural' perception: knowledge of them cannot be had without the aid of technological extensions of the nervous system" (LeClair, 1987: pp. 224–25).

Communications are global, and Jack is aware of this when he speaks to one of his ex-wives, now Mother Devi, from her ashram. He thinks, "Her tiny piping voice bounced down to me from a hollow ball in geosynchronous orbit" (WN, p. 260). For the most part, technology is viewed by the Gladneys as benevolent, perhaps best illustrated by Jack's visit to the ATM. He doesn't go there for money or to do any banking business, but for affirmation of his existence, countering his fear of death:

I went to the automated teller machine to check my balance. I inserted my card, entered my code, tapped out my request. The figure on the screen rough responded to my independent estimate, feebly arrived at after long searches through documents, tormented arithmetic. Waves of relief and gratitude flowed over me. The system had blessed my life. I felt its support and approval. The system hardware, the mainframe sitting in a locked room in some distant city. What a pleasing interaction. I sensed that something of deep personal value, but not money, not that at all, had been authenticated and confirmed. (WN, p. 46)

Even after his exposure to the toxic gas, a failure of technology, Jack looks to technology for the solution to both his fear of death and then to his exposure. As soon as he hears Winnie Richards' description of Dylar not as a pill but as a drug-delivery system with a polymer membrane and laser-drilled holes, he wants to have it for himself (WN, pp. 178–79). Jack is soon thinking about Dylar as the "benign counterpart of the Nyodene menace" (WN, p. 201). When he seeks advice from Murray after explaining about his presumably imminent death, Murray notes that technology is both the source and the solution of his problem: "You could put your faith in technology. It got you here, it can get you out. That is the whole point of technology. It creates an appetite for immortality on the one hand. It threatens universal extinction on the other. . . . New devices, new techniques every day. Lasers, masers, ultrasound. Give yourself up to it, Jack. Believe in it. They'll insert you in a gleaming tube, irradiate your body with the basic stuff of the universe. Light, energy, dreams. God's own goodness" (WN, p. 272).

Technology here is always double-edged, the poison and the antidote, the disease and the cure. For Jack and Babette, with their exaggerated fears of death, technology is the only way they can avoid both death and their debilitating phobia. Michael Valdez Moses has studied the strong connections between the role played by technology in WN and Martin Heidegger's writing on technology (an issue complicated by Heidegger's support of Nazism). "For DeLillo's characters, the immediate threat of death, brought on in some cases by the apparent failures of technology, may paradoxically serve a potentially redeeming function. The far greater danger is that technology may succeed in creating an illusion that it constitutes the only possible manner by which human beings apprehend themselves and their relationship to the world. The chief lure of technology, and its principal technique for domination over man's 'essence' . . . is its constantly reaffirmed promise of immortality" (Moses, 1991: p. 71).

Although he is a professor, Jack is thrown off by the exposure of the Nyodene. What it does is unclear; his main source of information throughout the Airborne Toxic Event is 14-year old Heinrich, who tracks the location of the cloud and the symptoms of the Nyodene gas by using his radio and binoculars, and who once saw a film about Nyodene in school. When he goes to the SIMUVAC technician, who has a computer that seems to be connected to all sources of information, Jack is at the mercy of the person who has the access to the advanced technology. Although he tries to be arch and evasive, Jack is subordinate to the young man, not a doctor or scientist, who is training for a simulated emergency by using a real emergency. The SIMUVAC technician looks into the computer screen and says,

"You're generating big numbers. . . . I tapped into your history. I'm getting bracketed numbers with pulsing stars." "What does that mean?" "You'd rather not know." (WN, p. 135). . . . "But you said we have a situation." "I didn't say it. The computer did. The whole system says it. It's what we call a massive data-base tally. Gladney, J. A. K. I punch in the name, the substance, the exposure time, and then I tap into your computer history. Your genetics, your personals, your medicals, your psychologicals, your police-and-hospitals. It comes back pulsing stars. That doesn't mean anything is going to happen to you as such, at least not today or tomorrow. It just means that you are the sum total of your data. No man escapes that." (WN, p. 136).

Jack never gets more information than this; the people who have access to computers and whatever information in the massive databases (Jack already has a "computer history," and must accept the facts revealed by his data). The person with a computer knows the meanings of the information, but the person with the apparently fatal exposure does not.

When Jack has his physical, his personal physician says, "I don't think I like your potassium very much at all," he went on. "Look here. A bracketed number with computerized stars." "What does that mean?" "There's no point in your knowing at this stage." . . . . "But is potassium the only thing I have to watch?" "The less you know the better" (WN, pp. 248–49). Similarly when Jack goes, at his doctor's request, for more tests at the ultra-high-tech medical facility with the rustic name, Autumn Harvest Farms, the technician says again, "I'm looking at bracket numbers with little stars" (WN, p. 266). He is supposed to bring back the results of his medical tests to his doctor without opening up the sealed reports and is told that the doctor knows how to read the codes. This is similar to Franz Kafka's story "The Penal Colony" in which the prison commandant's punishment machine inscribes the prisoner's crime on his back; all the other prisoners can see it and read it, but the prisoner who has committed the offense and is suffering the punishment cannot see what it says. Mark Conroy notes that, "If anything, the scientific advance chiefly on display in this world—the event itself, with its attendant SIMUVAC teams and medical studies—reduces the people further to infantilism, primitive fantasy, and dependence upon the system as if upon a deity. Indeed, throughout the novel, DeLillo charts a recursive movement whereby the large, impersonal forces of technology first produce death-dealing consequences and then offer themselves as palliatives to the fear of death they have aroused" (Conroy, 1994: p. 103; see also Keesey, 1993: pp. 145–46; Moses, 1991: p. 74).

Simulacra

Jean Baudrillard's concept of the *simulacra* has been mentioned repeatedly by critics and readers of *White Noise* (and it is a useful term for discussing a number of other works by DeLillo such as *Libra* and *Underworld*). "DeLillo differs from Baudrillard in one important respect. Baudrillard's position toward the postmodern world is ultimately one of radical skepticism: finally there is nothing outside the play of simulations, no real in which a radical critique of the simulational society might be grounded. DeLillo's writing, on the other hand, reveals a belief that fictional narrative can provide critical distance from, and a critical perspective on, the process it depicts" (Wilcox, 1991: p. 363).

The most apparent place of the simulation in *White Noise* is in the role played by SIMUVAC during the Airborne Toxic Event. Jack speaks with the technician about his group.

"What does SIMUVAC mean? Sounds important."

"Short for simulated evacuation. . . ."

"But this evacuation isn't simulated. It's real."

"We know that. But we thought we could use it as a model."

"A form of practice? Are you saying you saw a chance to use the real event in order to rehearse the simulation?"

"We took it right into the streets."

"How is it going?" I said.

"The insertion curve isn't as smooth as we would like. There's a probability excess. Plus, we don't have our victims laid out where we'd want them if this was an actual simulation." (*WN*, pp. 134–35).

This unit has computers and a brisk, efficient way; they are constantly training for all types of emergency situations, and they seem to have special, secret knowledge. They become a permanent part of Blacksmith, quietly doing their preparations, recruiting volunteers to act as victims so they can practice their scenarios of treatment and evacuation. Jack finds his daughter Steffie as one of the volunteer victims (WN, pp. 194–96). There is a SIMUVAC simulation of a noxious odor followed three days later by an actual noxious odor, but then even those who had participated in the SIMUVAC evacuation ignored the real noxious odor (WN, pp. 257–58), just as the Gladneys ignore their own shrieking smoke alarm and debate whether the fire trucks passing by their home with voices over loudspeakers ordering evacuation are serious.

But SIMUVAC and its activities are just part of the constant confusion of reality and the simulation. Jack describes the origins and development of his mask as J. A. K. Gladney with the bulky, dark glasses with heavy black frames: "I am the false character that follows the name around" (WN, pp. 16–17). The intellectual content of his Hitler Studies course focuses on the issues of propaganda, spectatorship, crowd manipulation through imagery, uniforms; although he has developed this area as his special disciplinary niche and has an international reputation. Jack doesn't speak German, and he doesn't always understand what his own lectures mean. The selection of Hitler was less an intellectual decision than it was a marketing move by his college chancellor and a career move for Jack. College-on-the-Hill pretends to be a college, the students pretend to be studying, and the faculty we see, Jack and the American Environments, are imposters (see Mark Conroy's comments on this; Conroy, 1994: p. 102). John Duvall has remarked that Jack is himself SIMUPROF (Duvall, 1994: p. 138).

Events are contrasted to the simulated versions; there are computer-generated voices, weather forecasts with satellite maps. Passengers on Bee's plane hear the pilot's voice over the loudspeaker when it seems as if they are going to crash: "Now we know what it's like. It is worse than we'd ever imagined. They didn't prepare us for this at the death simulator in Denver" (WN, p. 90). When Jack is in the

hospital being treated for his bullet wound by the German nun, although religion did not appear anywhere else in his thinking or activities during the book, he wants the nun to affirm the traditional
Catholic beliefs about heaven but she says, "Do you think we are
stupid?"

"Then what is heaven, according to the Church, if it isn't the
abode of God and the angels and the souls of those who are saved?"

"Saved? What is saved? This is a dumb head, who would come
in here to talk about angels. Show me an angel. Please. I want to
see."

He becomes increasingly insistent on what she should believe,
asks why she is dressed like a traditional nun and has kitschy pictures
of the Pope and John F. Kennedy clasping hands in heaven, and she
says with contempt that it is for "all the others who spend their lives
believing that *we* believe. . . . The devil, the angels, heaven, hell. If
we did not pretend to believe these things, the world would col-
lapse" (WN, pp. 302–3). As David Cowart notes, "The author toys
with a naive equation: we believe that the nuns believe. The nuns
are the signifiers of a divine signified. But in fact the nuns believe
only that we must believe that they believe: a circularity, which is
the circularity, the infinite deferral, of language itself" (Cowart,
2002: p. 86). This is SIMUFAITH (see Duvall, 1994: p. 138).

Another key example takes place when Jack is in the motel room
to shoot Willy Mink. Willy Mink's speech and thinking is completely intermixed with phrases and images from the television; he
doesn't separate himself from the voices on the television. One of
the symptoms of Dylar addiction is that words are taken for the real
items; Jack uses this against Willy Mink, saying "Hail of bullets," or
whispering "Fusillade" and causing Mink to drop to the floor, crawl-
ing away in terror, "childlike, miming, using principles of height-
ened-design but showing real terror, brilliant cringing fear" (WN, p.
297). This matches Baudrillard's notion of simulation in the con-

temporary: "The very definition of the real becomes: *that of which it is possible to give an equivalent reproduction.* . . . At the limit of this process of reproducibility, the real is not only what can be reproduced, but *that which is always already reproduced.* The hyperreal" (Baudrillard, 1983: p. 146). For Willy Mink, the understanding of "hail of bullets" derives from televised representations of shootings, just as Jack's approach to carrying out the murder is based on the *film noir* and the detective novel; until he is accidentally shot, he is following a mental script and acting in his own revenge-drama.

3

The Novel's Reception

On the whole, *White Noise* was well-received by reviewers. The handful who were very negative about the novel seem to have misread it entirely, looking for the traditional sort of narrative plot and characters that DeLillo never used in his first seven novels. Robert Phillips, for example, complains that the novel has been overwhelmed by the ideas and that there are no characters; what seem to be characters are only DeLillo's mouthpieces, and the work is boring (*America*, July 6–13, 1985: p. 16).

More typical was Thomas DePietro's notion of *White Noise* as a "Swiftian social satire." "From the accumulation of consumer rot, DeLillo manufactures a wonderfully comic apocalypse—a genuine revelation." Novelist Jay McInerney lavished praise on the book, calling it ". . . a stunning performance from one of our finest and most intelligent novelists. DeLillo's reach is broad and deep, combining acute observation of the textures of American life and analytic rigor." In McInerney's review, it is interesting to see the tension between a desire for traditional verisimilitude and the postmodern. He seems uncomfortable with the slide from realism to burlesque when DeLillo "gave all three of Gladney's wives CIA connections," and that DeLillo is perhaps too self-conscious in his shaping of the work. "But at his best," notes McInerney, "DeLillo masterfully orchestrates the idioms of pop culture" (*New Republic*, 142 [Feb. 4, 1985], p. 36). Another fiction writer, Jayne Anne Phillips, in her long, front-page piece in the *New York Times Book Review* (Jan. 13, 1985), cites the exactitude of DeLillo's reconstructions of interactions between parents and teenagers, like Jack's conversation with Heinrich where he tries to get Heinrich to say that it actually *is* raining although the radio did not say it was. "It is in documenting such epidemic evasiveness and apprehension, such lack of connection to the natural world and to technology, such bewilderment, that *White Noise* succeeds so brilliantly."

Some reviewers, while praising the power of the writing, the humor, the seriousness of the ideas or themes, and "virtuoso set pieces," have reservations about DeLillo's darkness and the lack of an answer to the problems and questions that the novel raises. Pico Iyer, in a long review, notes that "Next to DeLillo's large and terrifying talent, most modern fiction seems trifling indeed. A connoisseur of fear, he writes novels that leave a chill in one's bones. At the same time, however, it is always difficult to tell what he is about, beyond fear, emptiness, the dark." Iyer ends his review positively, warmed by the life inside the Gladney home and the fact that Jack is cheered by the sight of his children sleep. He judges *White Noise* to be a far greater book than *End Zone* "because it is something more than cold and curious reason; it offsets its existential shivers with a domestic strength that is touching and true" (*Partisan Review*, 53 [1986], rptd. in Mark Osteen's critical edition of *WN*).

4

The Novel's Performance

There have been no film or television adaptations of *White Noise*, though it has been rumored to be under option for films almost since its publication. But now that the film rights for *Underworld* have reportedly been sold for more than one million dollars, perhaps we will soon have *White Noise* glowing from television screens, appropriately, the stray fragments of dialogue and different voices, pieces of advertisements, leaking into the hallways and through the walls of middle-class family homes.

Since the publication of *Underworld*, *White Noise* is referred to as DeLillo's "breakthrough" book, the novel that gave him a secure place in the canon of contemporary American fiction writers, while *Underworld* is his prolix masterpiece. DeLillo's reputation is such that when the sponsors of the most prestigious award for fiction in Britain, The Booker Prize, announced that they were planning to change the eligibility rules so that American fiction could be considered, in addition to British, Irish, and Commonwealth fiction, the current chair of judges objected strongly. Professor Lisa Jardine "expressed concern that the subtle character of British and Commonwealth writing could be overwhelmed by American competition, suggesting, for example, that writers of the power and scope of Philip Roth and Don DeLillo would beat all comers" (*Publisher's Weekly*, May 28, 2002).

White Noise has been republished in Penguin's "Great Books of the Twentieth Century," a short list that includes the obvious modernists: Joseph Conrad's *Heart of Darkness*, James Joyce's *A Portrait of the Artist as a Young Man*, and Marcel Proust's *Swann's Way*, but also such appropriate contemporaries of DeLillo's work as Thomas Pynchon's *Gravity's Rainbow* (1973) and Salman Rushdie's *Midnight's Children* (1980). As another sign of the current status of the novel, *White Noise* has also been republished in the Viking Critical Library as *White Noise: Text and Criticism* edited by Mark Osteen (1998).

With the popularity of *White Noise* in the university community, it is not surprising that it has already influenced a very substantial body of criticism devoted just to this work, or in connection with DeLillo's other works. Although *Libra* and *Underworld* (and perhaps DeLillo's next novel, *Cosmopolis*, announced but not yet published at the time of this writing) cause the place of *White Noise* to shift in status within DeLillo's canon, the latter will still be considered a major work. We can just indicate a few works here that might be especially useful as a starting point in studying the work.

Most readers of *White Noise*, the casual, one-time readers (if such readers can be found, somehow restraining themselves from reading the novel again and again), will be content with the standard text. But the reader with a more scholarly, critical interest will certainly want to read Osteen's brilliant edition. It has a brief introduction and DeLillo chronology, and then the full text of the novel. The next section, "Contexts," includes excerpts from interviews with DeLillo and a few carefully selected pages each from *Americana*, *End Zone*, and *Players*, and, in full, DeLillo's essay on Hitler, anti-Semitism, and the attraction of apocalyptic millenarianism (first published in 1989). Then there are stories about the Bhopal disaster, reprinted from *Newsweek* magazine. There are four book reviews, and then a generous collection of seven critical essays, topics for discussion and papers, and a bibliography. The Osteen critical edition is currently available in an inexpensive paperback format. Its existence is testimony both to the esteem that has accrued to DeLillo generally and to this novel in particular, and to the frequent inclusion of this novel in university courses.

There are two convenient collections of key essays, both edited by Frank Lentricchia. One covers many of DeLillo's works, and its title, *Introducing Don DeLillo* (Duke University Press, 1996; it is a reprint of a special issue of *South Atlantic Quarterly* from 1991), indicates how suddenly DeLillo seemed to grow in stature. The critical articles are all lively and informative; particularly relevant for *White Noise* are the pieces by Eugene Goodheart and John Frow. The longer version of the Anthony DeCurtis interview with DeLillo also appears here. The one drawback to the collection is that there are no notes, page numbers, or sources for the many quotations. The other volume is the slim *New Essays on* White Noise (Cambridge University Press, 1991), with very useful articles by Thomas J. Ferraro, Paul Cantor, Michael Valdez Moses, and Frank Lentricchia.

There have not been very many monographs on Don DeLillo, but readers of *White Noise* would benefit from reading three: Tom LeClair's pioneering 1987 study, *In the Loop: Don DeLillo and the Systems Novel* (University of Illinois Press; exploring the way DeLillo's novels are placed in the general culture, the intellectual contexts of his work, the structural metaphors of loops and circles as methods of reading and writing, and the appropriation of systems theory or "communications of ecological systems, including man"); Mark Osteen's complex and exciting *American Magic and Dread: Don De-Lillo's Dialogue with Culture* (University of Pennsylvania Press, 2000), a work of cultural studies that covers all of DeLillo's novels through *Underworld* with particular emphasis on the issues of media, waste, and consumerism and commodification. Another excellent and very recent book is David Cowart's *Don DeLillo: The Physics of Language* (Athens: University of Georgia Press, 2002), which applies modernist, postmodernist, and post-structuralist language theories to all of DeLillo's novels through *The Body Artist*. None of these three books are simple in their approaches or theories, but they are particularly valuable for readers with some background in critical theory. They are all knowledgeable, well-written, and illuminating.

Further Resources and Discussion Questions

Web-sites

There are some excellent web-sites devoted to DeLillo. The two most important are:

1. The Don DeLillo Society: <http://www.ksu.edu/english/nelp/delillo> This is the official site of the scholarly organization for the study and discussion of DeLillo's work. The site has an extensive bibliography, calls-for-papers, announcements of events, and news about DeLillo and his publications and activities. There is an e-mail listserv for members of the Society.
2. Don DeLillo's America: <http://perival.com/delillo/delillo.html> This site has DeLillo biography, bibliography, and separate pages on all of DeLillo's works, criticism, reviews, interviews, events, news, and extensive links.

Discussion and Paper Ideas

We have mentioned Walter Benjamin's essay "The Work of Art in the Age of Mechanical Reproduction" and the concept of the "aura" in connection with "The Most Photographed Barn in America" and

Babette's attempt to de-glamorize television. Read Benjamin's essay and consider the connections made in that essay between reproducibility of art and the Fascist aesthetics of the spectacle. How is this related to Jack's teaching of Hitler and Nazism, to Murray Siskind's analysis of the supermarket, and to the way the media permeates the lives of the Gladneys and the other characters?

Analyze the last chapter of *White Noise*. Does it have closure? Is there an ending to the plot? Is there a plot? Would you characterize the ending as hopeful and optimistic, the worst having passed (the toxic cloud, the discovery of Babette's infidelity, Jack's turn to violent revenge in attempting to kill Willy Mink, and so on)? Or is the ending gloomy and pessimistic (we are left with the technology that produced Nyodene-D, Dylar, and whatever it is that caused people to sicken at the school, the men in Mylex suits still in the area, the sunsets suddenly brighter and more spectacular, death has entered Jack)? What are the unanswered plot questions in the novel? How do you understand the final image of the supermarket and the tabloids?

For a contemporary American novel, *White Noise* is surprisingly and perhaps strangely lacking in representation or discussion of sexuality. Even though we see the Gladneys in bed, they are distracted from sex by their death fears and by rummaging around their basement in the accumulation of magazines for sexually stimulating material to read to each other. Murray Siskind gets involved with a prostitute during the Airborne Toxic Event, but he wants to pay her to let him pretend to save her from choking by using the Heimlich maneuver. Although Babette confesses to having visited Willy Mink in his hotel to have sex in exchange for Dylar, this is hardly imaginable given Willy Mink's almost complete dementia. What is the place of sexuality in contemporary America, as shown in *White Noise*? If it does not appear, why not? How does DeLillo treat sexuality in his other novels?

A related issue is that of violence. Under what forms does violence appear in *White Noise* and what analysis does violence receive by the two major cultural interpreters in the work, Jack and Murray? The violence of Hitler and the Nazi era is always in the background, of course, but entirely unacknowledged by Jack. Heinrich plays chess through correspondence with an imprisoned mass-murderer. Jack's father-in-law gives him an illegal, untraceable gun and Jack feels transformed: "A loaded weapon, How quickly it worked a change in me. . . . Did Vernon mean to provoke thought, provide my life with a fresh design, a scheme, a shapeliness?" (*WN*, p. 241). As soon as Babette tells Jack about her visits to the motel to trade sex for Dylar, she expects Jack will seek a violent revenge. Timothy Melley has remarked that Murray's statement, "Violence is a form of rebirth," virtually quotes "Richard Slotkin's classic description of masculine self-making as 'regeneration through violence,'" and Melley points out this "familiar form of masculine agency recovery is one of DeLillo's obsessions" (*Empire of Conspiracy: The Culture of Paranoia in Postwar America* [Ithaca NY: Cornell University Press, 2000], 148). How does violence operate in *White Noise*?

Umberto Eco's *Travels in Hyperreality* and Jean Baudrillard's *America* both offer critical European views of American culture (from different perspectives, Eco a cultural semiotician and Baudrillard a postmodern philosopher writing from a Marxist background). When DeLillo returned from several years in Europe, he was moved by the changes he noticed in America, after such a long absence, to begin *White Noise*. Read these two studies and compare their critique of American consumerism, possessions, values, towns and landscapes, and the media (especially television and movies) with DeLillo's critique in *White Noise*.

How does the imagery and issues of waste and pollution appear throughout DeLillo's novels from *End Zone* through *Underworld*? DeLillo often uses the technique of cataloging, making page-long lists of garbage, often unexpectedly, such as the long catalogue of paper items the fans toss onto the baseball field in the middle of the key game in *Underworld*. How do such catalogues function thematically? How do they impact readers emotionally?

Compare these displays and analyses of waste to those of other novelists who repeatedly explore this area, including a contemporary author who has earned DeLillo's respect, Thomas Pynchon (especially in *The Crying of Lot 49* and *Gravity's Rainbow*). It might be a useful tool, in such an exploration, to read some of the works in "eco-criticism," and to see how such critics approach DeLillo's work. In particular, read Richard Kerridge's "Small Rooms and the Ecosystem: Environmentalism and DeLillo's *White Noise*," in *Writing the Environment: Ecocriticism and Literature*, ed. R. Kerridge and Neil Sammells [London: Zed, 1998], pp. 182–95, and Dana Phillips, "Don DeLillo's Postmodern Pastoral," in *Reading the Earth: New Directions in the Study of Literature and the Environment*, ed. Michael Branch, et al [Moscow, Idaho: University of Idaho Press, 1998], 235–46).

Bibliography

1. WORKS BY DON DELILLO

Novels

Americana (Boston: Houghton Mifflin, 1971).

End Zone (Boston: Houghton Mifflin, 1972).

Great Jones Street (Boston: Houghton Mifflin, 1973).

Ratner's Star (New York: Knopf, 1976).

Players (New York: Knopf, 1977).

Running Dog (New York: Knopf, 1978).

Amazons (New York: Holt, Rinehart, and Winston, 1980) [a collaboration, under the pseudonym Cleo Birdwell].

The Names (New York: Knopf, 1982).

White Noise (New York: Viking, 1985).

Libra (New York: Viking, 1988).

Mao II (New York: Viking, 1991).

Underworld (New York: Scribner, 1997).

The Body Artist (New York: Scribner, 2001).

Cosmopolis (New York: Scribner, announced for publication in April, 2003).

Plays

"The Engineer of Moonlight," *Cornell Review* 5 (Winter, 1979), pp. 21–47.

The Day Room (New York: Knopf, 1987; premiered at American Repertory Theatre, Cambridge MA, 1986).

Valparaiso (New York: Touchstone, 1999; premiered at American Repertory Theatre, Cambridge MA, 1999).

"The Rapture of the Athlete Assumed into Heaven" (two-page play premiered at American Repertory Theatre, Cambridge MA, 1990, as part of festival of one-minute plays, published in *South Atlantic Quarterly* 91.2 (Spring, 1992), pp. 241–42.

"The Mystery at the Middle of Ordinary Life" (two-page play), *Zoetrope* 4.4 (2000).

Stories

"The River Jordan," *Epoch* 10.2 (Winter, 1960), pp. 105–20.

"Take the 'A' Train," *Epoch* 12.1 (Spring, 1962), pp. 9–25.

"Spaghetti and Meatballs," *Epoch* 14.3 (Spring, 1965), pp. 244–50.

"Coming Sun. Mon. Tues." *Kenyon Review* 28.3 (June, 1966), pp. 391–94.

"Baghdad Towers West," *Epoch* 17 (1968), pp. 195–217.

"The Uniforms," *Carolina Quarterly* 22.1 (Winter, 1970), pp. 4–11.

"In the Men's Room of the Sixteenth Century," *Esquire* (Dec., 1971), pp. 174–77, 243, 246.

"Total Loss Weekend," *Sports Illustrated* (Nov. 27, 1972), pp. 98–101.

"Creation," *Antaeus* 33 (1979), pp. 32–46.

"Human Moments in World War III," *Esquire* (July, 1983), pp. 118–26.

"The Ivory Acrobat," *Granta* 25 (Autumn, 1988), pp. 199–212.

"The Runner," *Harper's* (Sept., 1988), pp. 61–63.

"Pafko at the Wall," *Harper's* (Oct., 1992), pp. 35–70 (this became the prologue to the novel *Underworld* [1997] and was published as separate novella in 2001 by Scribner).

"The Angel Esmeralda," *Esquire* (May, 1994), pp. 100–9 (reprinted in *Best American Short Stories 1995*), integrated into *Underworld*.

"Baader-Meinhof," *New Yorker* (April 1, 2002), pp. 78–82.

Essays

"American Blood: A Journey Through the Labyrinth of Dallas and JFK," *Rolling Stone* (Dec. 8, 1983), pp. 21–28, 74.

"The Artist Naked in Cage," speech delivered at the New York Public Library's event for Human Rights in China, called "Stand in for Wei Jingsheng." Short version published in *New Yorker* (May 26, 1997), pp. 6–7. Full version online at "Human Rights in China" web-site.

"In the Ruins of the Future," *Harper's* (Dec., 2001), pp. 33–40. [on Sept 11, 2001, terrorist events, terrorism, technology, and the impact on America.]

"The Power of History," *New York Times Magazine* (Sept. 7, 1997), pp. 60–63.

"Silhouette City: Hitler, Manson, and the Millenium," *Dimensions* 4.3 (1989), pp. 29–34. rptd. in Mark Osteen's critical edition of *WN*.

Interviews

Arensberg, Ann. "Seven Seconds [interview with Don DeLillo]," *Vogue* (August, 1988), pp. 337–39, 390.

Begley, Adam. "The Art of Fiction CXXXV," *Paris Review* 128 (1993), pp. 274–306.

DeCurtis, Anthony. "'An Outsider in this Society': An Interview with Don DeLillo," in Frank Lentricchia, ed. *Introducing Don DeLillo* (Durham: Duke University Press, 1991), pp. 43–66.

Howard, Gerald. "The American Strangeness: An Interview with Don De-Lillo," *Hungry Mind Review* 43 (Fall, 1997), pp. 13–16.

LeClair, Thomas. "An Interview with Don DeLillo," *Contemporary Literature* 23 (1982), pp. 19–31.

McAuliffe, Jody. "Interview with Don DeLillo," *South Atlantic Quarterly* 99.2–3 (Apring/Summer, 2000), pp. 609–15.

Nadotti, Maria. "An Interview with Don DeLillo," *Salmagundi* 100 (Fall, 1993), pp. 86–97.

2. SECONDARY WORKS

Aubry, Timothy. "*White Noise* Generation," *Critical Matrix*12.1–2 (Fall 2000-Spring, 2001), pp. 148–73.

Baudrillard, Jean. *Simulations* (New York: Semiotext(e), 1983).

Baudrillard, Jean. *Selected Writings*, ed. Mark Poster (Stanford: Stanford University Press, 1988).

Benjamin, Walter. "The Storyteller" (pp. 83–109) and "The Work of Art in the Age of Mechanical Reproduction" (pp. 217–251), both in his *Illuminations*, ed. Hannah Arendt (New York: Schocken Books, 1969).

Billy, Ted. "The Externalization of the Self in American Life: Don DeLillo's *White Noise*," *Journal of Evolutionary Psychology* 19.3–4 (Aug., 1998), pp. 270–83.

Bonca, Cornel. "Don DeLillo's *White Noise*: The Natural Language of the Species," *College Literature* 23.2 (June, 1996), pp. 25–44, rptd. in Osteen *WNTC*.

Cantor, Paul A. "'Adolf, We Hardly Knew You,'" in Frank Lentricchia, ed., *New Essays: White Noise* (Cambridge: Cambridge University Press, 1991), pp. 39–62.

Caton, Lou F. "Romanticism and the Postmodern Novel: Three Scenes from Don DeLillo's *White Noise*," *English Language Notes* 35.1 (Sept., 1997), pp. 38–48.

Conroy, Mark. "From Tombstone to Tabloid: Authority Figured in *White Noise*," *Critique: Studies in Contemporary Fiction* 35.2 (Winter, 1994), pp. 97–110.

Cowart, David. *Don DeLillo: The Physics of Language* (University of Georgia Press, 2002).

Deitering, Cynthia. "The Postnatural Novel: Toxic Consciousness in Fiction of the 1980s," in Cheryll Glotfelty and Harold Fromm, eds., *The Ecocriticism Reader: Landmarks in Literary Ecology* (Athens GA: University of Georgia Press, 1996), pp. 196–203.

doCormo, Stephen N. "Subjects, Objects, and the Postmodern Differend in Don DeLillo's *White Noise*," *Lit: Literature Interpretation Theory* 11.1 (July, 2000), pp. 1–33.

Duvall, John N. "The (Super) Marketplace of Images: Television as Unmediated Mediation in DeLillo's *White Noise*," *Arizona Quarterly* 50.3

(Autumn, 1994), pp. 127–53, rptd. in Mark Osteen's critical edition of WN.

Duvall, John. *Don DeLillo's* Underworld: *A Reader's Guide* (New York: Continuum, 2002).

Engles, Tim. "'Who Are You, Literally?': Fantasies of the White Self in *White Noise*," *Modern Fiction Studies* 45.3 (Fall, 1999), pp. 755–87.

Ferraro, Thomas J. "Whole Families Shopping At Night!" in Frank Lentricchia, ed., *New Essays: White Noise* (Cambridge: Cambridge University Press, 1991), pp. 15–38.

Frow, John. "The Last Things Before the Last: Notes on *White Noise*," *South Atlantic Quarterly* 89.2 (Spring, 1990), pp. 413–29. [reprinted in Lentricchia, *Introducing DD*; also rptd. in *Osteen WNTC*.

Green, Jeremy. "Disaster Footage: Spectacles of Violence in DeLillo's Fiction," *Modern Fiction Studies* 45.3 (1999), pp. 571–99.

Hantke, Steffen. *Conspiracy and Paranoia in Contemporary American Fiction: The Works of Don DeLillo and Joseph McElroy* (Frankfurt: Peter Lang, 1994).

Hayles, N. Katherine. "Postmodern Parataxis: Embodied Texts, Weightless Information," *American Literary History* 2.3 (Fall, 1990), pp. 394–421.

Heffernan, Teresa. "Can the Apocalypse Be Post?" in Richard Dellamora, ed., *Postmodern Apocalypse: Theory and Cultural Practice at the End* (Philadelphia: University of Pennsylvania Press, 1995), pp. 171–81.

Heller, Arno. "Simulacrum vs. Death: An American Dilemma in Don DeLillo's *White Noise*," in Elisabeth Kraus and Carolin Auer, eds., *Simulacrum America: The USA and the Popular Media* (Rochester NY: Camden House, 2000), pp. 37–48.

Keesey, Douglas. *Don DeLillo* (New York: Twayne, 1993).

Kerridge, Richard. "Small Rooms and the Ecosystem: Environmentalism and DeLillo's *White Noise*," in Richard Kerridge and Neil Sammells, eds., *Writing the Environment: Ecocriticism and Literature* (London: Zed, 1998), pp. 182–95.

King, Noel. "Reading *White Noise*: Floating Remarks," *Critical Quarterly* 33.3 (Autumn, 1991), pp. 66–83.

LeClair, Tom. *In the Loop: Don DeLillo and the Systems Novel* (Urbana: University of Illinois Press, 1987).

Lentricchia, Frank, ed. *Introducing Don DeLillo* (Durham: Duke University Press, 1991).

Lentricchia, Frank, ed., *New Essays on White Noise* (Cambridge: Cambridge University Press, 1991).

Lentricchia, Frank. "Tales of the Electronic Tribe," in Frank Lentricchia, ed., *New Essays: White Noise* (Cambridge: Cambridge University Press, 1991), pp. 87–113.

Leps, Marie-Christine. "Empowerment through Information: A Discursive Critique," *Cultural Critique*, 31 (Fall, 1995), pp. 179–96.

Maltby, Paul. "The Romantic Metaphysics of Don DeLillo," *Contemporary Literature* 37.2 (Summer, 1996), pp. 258–77. [reprinted in Mark Osteen's critical edition of *White Noise*].

Melley, Timothy. *Empire of Conspiracy: The Culture of Paranoia in Postwar America* (Ithaca: Cornell University Press, 2000).

Messmer, Michael W. "'Thinking it through completely': The Interpretation of Nuclear Culture," *Centennial Review* 32.4 (Fall, 1988), pp. 397–413.

Moses, Michael Valdez. "Lust Removed from Nature," in Frank Lentricchia, ed., *New Essays: White Noise* (Cambridge: Cambridge University Press, 1991), pp. 63–86.

Muirhead, Marion. "Deft Acceleration: The Occult Geometry of Time in *White Noise*," *Critique: Studies in Contemporary Fiction* 42.4 (Summer, 2001), pp. 402–15.

Osteen, Mark, ed., Don DeLillo, *White Noise: Text and Criticism* (New York: Penguin, 1998). [WNTC]

Osteen, Mark. *American Magic and Dread: Don DeLillo's Dialogue with Culture* (Philadelphia: University of Pennsylvania Press, 2000).

Pastore, Judith Laurence. "Palomar and Gladney: Calvino and DeLillo Play with the Dialectics of Subject/Object Relationships," *Italian Culture* 9 (1991), pp. 331–42.

Peyser, Thomas. "Globalization in America: The Case of Don DeLillo's *White Noise*," *CLIO* 25.3 (Spring, 1996), pp. 255–71.

Phillips, Dana. "Don DeLillo's Postmodern Pastoral," in Michael Branch, et al, eds., *Reading the Earth: New Directions in the Study of Literature and Environment* (Moscow: University of Idaho Press, 1998), pp. 235–46.

Pifer, Ellen. *Demon or Doll: Images of the Child in Contemporary Writing and Culture* (Charlottesville: University Press of Virginia, 2000).

Reeve, N. H. and Richard Kerridge. "Toxic Events: Postmodernism and DeLillo's *White Noise*," *Cambridge Quarterly* 23.4 (1994), pp. 303–23.

Rump, Keiran. "The Wilder State in DeLillo's *White Noise*," *Notes on Contemporary Literature* 30.2 (March, 2000), pp. 10–12.

Ruthrof, Horst. "Narrative and the Digital: On the Syntax of the Postmodern," *AUMLA: Journal of the Australasian Universities Language and Literature Association* 74 (Nov., 1990), pp. 185–200.

Saltzman, Arthur M. "The Figure in the Static: *White Noise*," *Modern Fiction Studies* 40.4 (Winter, 1994), pp. 807–26, rptd. in Mark Osteen's critical edition of *WN*.

Salyer, Gregory. "Myth, Magic, and Dread: Reading Culture Religiously," *Literature & Theology* 9.3 (Sept., 1995), pp. 261–77.

Soltan, Margaret. "From Black Magic to White Noise: Malcolm Lowry and Don DeLillo," in Frederick Asals and Paul Tuessen, eds., *A Darkness that Murmured: Essays on Malcolm Lowry and the Twentieth Century* (Toronto: University of Toronto Press, 2000), pp. 200–22.

Walker, Joseph S. "Criminality, the Real, and the Story of America: The Case of Don DeLillo," *Centennial Review* 43.3 (Fall, 1999), pp. 433–66.

Weinstein, Arnold. *Nobody's Home: Speech, Self, and Place in American Fiction from Hawthorne to DeLillo* (New York: Oxford University Press, 1993), chapter 14: "Don DeLillo: Rendering the Words of the Tribe," pp. 288–315.

Whalan, Mark. "The Literary Detective in Postmodernity," *Paradoxa: Studies in World Literary Genres* 4.9 (1998), pp. 119–33.

Wilcox, Leonard. "Baudrillard, DeLillo's *White Noise*, and the End of Heroic Narrative," *Contemporary Literature* 32.3 (Fall, 1991), pp. 346–65.

Zimmerman, Lee. "Public and Potential Space: Winnicott, Ellison, and DeLillo," *Centennial Review* 43.3 (Fall, 1999), pp. 565–74.

Reviews of White Noise

Adams, Phoebe-Lou. *The Atlantic* 255 (Feb., 1985), p. 100.

DePietro, Thomas. *Commonweal* 112 (April 5, 1985), p. 219.

Iyer, Pico. "A Connoisseur of Fear," *Partisan Review* 53 (1986), rptd. in Mark Osteen's critical edition of WN.

Disch, Thomas M. *The Nation* 240 (Feb. 2, 1985), p. 120.

Johnson, Diane. "Conspirators," *The New York Review of Books* 32 (March 14, 1985), p. 6. rptd. in Mark Osteen's critical edition of WN.

Lhamon, W. T. *Library Journal* 110 (Feb. 1, 1985), p. 112.

McInerney, Jay. *The New Republic* 192 (Feb. 4, 1985), p. 36.

Mobillo, Albert. "Death by Inches," *Village Voice* (April 30, 1985), rptd. in Mark Osteen's critical edition of WN.

Phillips, Jayne Anne. *The New York Times Book Review* (Jan. 13, 1985), p. 1.

Phillips, Robert. *America* 153 (July 6–13, 1985), p. 16.

Shapiro, Anna. *Saturday Review* 11 (Mar.-April, 1985), p. 65.

Sheppard, R. Z. *Time* 125 (Jan. 21, 1985), p. 71.

Yurick, Sol. "Fleeing Death in a World of Hyper-Babble," *Philadelphia Quarterly* (Jan. 20, 1985), rptd. in Mark Osteen's critical edition of WN.